D1569876

Career Launcher

Finance

Career Launcher series

Career Launcher

Finance

Suzanne Northington

Ferguson's
An Infobase Learning Company
Elgin Community College
Library

Career Launcher: **Finance**

Copyright © 2011 by Infobase Learning, Inc.

Ferguson's
An imprint of Infobase Learning
132 West 31st Street
New York NY 10001

Library of Congress Cataloging-in-Publication Data

Suzanne Northington.
    Finance / by Suzanne Northington.
        p. cm.—(The career launcher series)
    Includes bibliographical references and index.
    ISBN-13: 978-0-8160-7952-0 (hardcover : alk. paper)
    ISBN-10: 0-8160-7952-8 (hardcover : alk. paper)
1. Finance—Vocational guidance. 2. Financial services industry—
Vocational guidance. 3. Investment advisors. I. Title.
    HG173.N74 2011
    332—dc23

                                                        2011018196

Ferguson's books are available at special discounts when purchased in bulk quantities for businesses, associations, institutions, or sales promotions. Please call our Special Sales Department in New York at (212) 967-8800 or (800) 322-8755.

You can find Ferguson's on the World Wide Web at
http://www.infobaselearning.com

Produced by Print Matters, Inc.
Text design by A Good Thing, Inc.
Cover design by Takeshi Takahashi
Cover printed by Yurchak Printing, Landisville, Pa.
Book printed and bound by Yurchak Printing, Landisville, Pa.
Date printed: October 2011

Printed in the United States of America

10 9 8 7 6 5 4 3 2 1

This book is printed on acid-free paper.

Contents

Foreword

The finance industry spans such a large cross section of career opportunities that it now attracts a significant number of college graduates who have completed varying fields of study. For example, armed with an undergraduate degree in marketing from the University of Colorado, I entered the MBA program at the Marshall School of Business at the University of Southern California (USC). I had no aspirations at the time of entering the finance field; however, I was always interested in my finance classes.

USC was one of the first programs to offer a course in portfolio management and I was fortunate enough to be awarded one of the seats. The course was unique at the time because one of the local investment management firms had created a fund specifically for students to trade so that they could receive hands on experience in portfolio management. Our professor taught modern portfolio theory and also was an early proponent of the Chartered Financial Analyst (CFA) designation. As talented as he was, it was still nearly impossible to connect the dots between what he was teaching and how it related to constructing a portfolio. All we wanted to do was pick stocks and watch eagerly as their value appreciated. We fumbled through the concepts of diversification and Dr. William Sharpe's Capital Asset Pricing Model and interviewed with the brokerage firms that recruited on campus.

This narrow view of the finance industry has been significantly broadened at campuses across the world. Students today not only can study portfolio management, but also financial engineering and asset class focused investing. There is a broad understanding of the difference between institutional and retail investing. One thing is constant however; theory and practice are still far apart.

I have spent my entire career trying to explain to friends and family who are not in the financial services profession what it is exactly that I do. I can never explain it fully in one simple sentence. Most people think of a career in finance from a brokerage perspective only. People often ask me which stocks they should invest in and my response is always, "I have no idea."

I began my career at Wilshire Associates, my first (and present) employer as a newly minted MBA in Finance and Entrepreneurship. The theory was on the surface but entering the world of billions rather than thousands was daunting and I immediately knew I needed to supplement my MBA with a CFA if I was going to keep up with my extremely experienced and quantitatively-focused colleagues.

I was fortunate to land a position at a firm that serves institutional investors. Wilshire was founded by scientists and individuals with PhDs in finance at the very genesis of the institutional finance industry. The passage of the Employee Retirement Income Security Act (ERISA) in 1974 directed how corporate retirement plans had to administer and oversee their assets. This single piece of legislation changed the finance industry forever and continues to be the foundation of fiduciary principles for nearly all pools of assets.

The range of employment opportunities at Wilshire covered many facets of the finance field. These positions included modeling portfolio risk, developing performance attribution models, programming, performance measurement, investment manager selection, investment structure, asset allocation, index construction, and asset management.

There were so many opportunities in exciting areas; it was often difficult to choose. Two things were certain: it was a hard-driving culture and seeing daylight was optional. Today when I interview candidates, I'm looking for one main thing: character. The specific skills for a particular position can be taught, but you cannot instill a drive to succeed, or a willingness to work harder than anyone else to achieve common goals. When you find THAT candidate with those characteristics, you hire them on the spot.

Wilshire was and is a very nimble firm with plentiful opportunities for those willing to take risks. The early years of a career are your training wheels; you can take risks and reach beyond your comfort zone. Fear of failure should not be even in your thought process. When I look back at that early part of my career at Wilshire, I think RISK in capital letters. However, I'm sure my friends and family thought STUPID in capital letters.

I naturally gravitated towards an area at Wilshire whose mission was to expand our borders out of the United States. Before I could blink, I was exploring underdeveloped countries to seek introductions to their capital markets. The opening of a new market is very exciting and traveling to South America, Africa, both Southern and Northern Asia, and the Middle East in the early 1990s was truly "out there" on the investment frontier. I was in my mid-twenties and, for the most part, traveling alone and not speaking the native language anywhere.

After spending several years introducing our clients to their counterparts in the emerging markets, I was asked to open our first office outside of the U.S. Another risk taken, as I was to move to London and begin build a client base. Once I had that started, I could plant a flag and start hiring employees and begin my first foray into management. It was like starting a business within a business. As any new business owner will tell you, the lines between doing and managing are always a bit blurry. Thinking of my earlier statement, fear of failure was like the proverbial monkey on my back: it drove me to push myself beyond what I thought I was capable of and taught me about the importance of having a competent team.

Prior to my London experience, I thought that if I worked really hard and was reasonably smart, I could succeed through sheer will. Once you begin to build something, you realize that it is not about you at all, but about building something that can exist and last without you. Back in the Wilshire headquarters in Santa Monica, California, there were incredible colleagues who were ready to support me eight time zones away around the clock. Building a team that was as equally competent was paramount to the success of our new office. I could bring the clients in like no one else, but it took my successor, who knew how to delegate much better that did I, to transition the office to stand on its own.

Back stateside, I was asked to run U.S. client service for Wilshire's Analytics Group. This experience provided me with the opportunity to work on my management skills and to continue to hone my client service skills. I had hired our London team and also initiated terminations (something at which I never set out to be proficient); however, now I did not have to worry about running the office, or operations or sales. I could focus on growing the client service teams and product development and, most importantly, client satisfaction, which is a function of the first two responsibilities. Growing client service teams is really a study of people and their capabilities. Managing employees requires that you have strong observation skills so that you can promote their strengths and compensate for their weaknesses. It also requires that you understand your own. A hiring mistake is very costly both in terms of time and dollars, and it is very important that the decision to hire is well thought out and not rushed.

The financial markets keep everyone on their toes. You can learn all of the investment theory out there and half the time your assumptions will be wrong. Market cycles, however, are great predictors of the job market. The 1980s were the era of the investment banker. The 1990s brought huge growth to traditional long-only investment managers and private equity. The early 2000s were dominated by alternative managers, specifically hedge funds. The employment opportunities and the candidate pool that wanted to fill those opportunities followed that cycle.

Now we are faced with one of the most challenging job markets in recent history. The financial industry is for the most part driven by asset-based fees. Which means good times when markets are up and Armageddon after the last 18 months. Jobs are as plentiful as the assets when the equity markets in particular are having a good run.

Towards the end of the Tech or "TMT" ("telecom, media, and technology", as it is affectionately called in the financial world) bubble, most financial firms that operated in the middle of the compensation pack had difficulties keeping the lights on, as you could not pay entry-level candidates enough to keep them interested in the firm. This new army of 22-year-old undergraduates would arrive at the door with expectations of above market salaries and exorbitant signing bonuses for positions that literally paid 50 to 60 percent less the year before. We could count on them to stick around for six months, maybe up to a year, before they were off to their next opportunity. Add the elevated cost of compensation to the job training costs that were expended from the constant hiring/departure cycle and the only folks that were truly enjoying themselves were the Executive Search firms.

If it was not for the carnage of the assets that occurred as a result of the market crash, you would have heard an audible sigh of relief from most employers after the bursting of the employment bubble that was created from the market bubble. As firms began to shed their excess employees, hiring practices began to normalize. However, then we began to see a "new generation" of candidates that were either a byproduct of the frothy markets or some type of "me" phenomenon.

As the markets began to gear up for another prolonged period of positive returns in 2003, a new kind of candidate emerged. These candidates, both undergraduate and graduate, did not ask what they could do for their company but what their company could do for them. These candidates when hired were very concerned that we respect the boundaries between work and their personal time. The work ethic went missing in action and we were left with a "productivity" problem. The easy answer was to only hire candidates who understood and honored deadlines. My belief is that this new group was young from a maturity standpoint. They went from helicopter parents to college to graduate school and had not been taught basic skills such as punctuality. After a little corporate tough love and a few years of seasoning, this group is starting to step up.

We read everywhere that high schools are not preparing students for college, and that colleges must now provide remedial classes to allow these students to catch up. If candidates have no previous work experience then it is up to their new employers to train them not only how to do their job but also how to behave at their job. My father taught me five main principles to succeeding in business: 1.) Never watch the clock; be the first to arrive and the last to leave. 2.) Never keep score. 3.) No one should ever have to tell you what to do. 4.) The customer/client is always right. 5.) A fool and his money soon part. These ideas can and have been stated many different ways; as obvious as they may seem, many candidates begin their careers without a foundation of how to approach the work environment.

Directly after the GFC (I was recently informed that the "global financial crisis" now has an official acronym), I would receive unsolicited resumes from candidates that were much more experienced than the position required. They were also willing to take a substantial pay cut to maintain employment. Many of these candidates were refugees from Wall Street and using their current employment status to take their careers in a different direction. The market seems to have absorbed most of these individuals and the current pool of candidates that we see seems to be focused on particular segments of the market place. Many have worked at failed hedge funds. Today's candidate receives much more practical training in business school for careers in the finance field. There also are numerous designations that may be earned to supplement areas that require more depth such as the CFA, the Chartered Alternative Investment Analyst (CAIA) and the Financial Risk Manager (FRM), to name a few.

Any additional skill that a candidate brings to an interview will be noticed. We are looking for the whole package—someone who has the investment skills, presentation skills, writing skills, software application skills, and presence with colleagues and clients. A candidate that walks in the door with the confidence and character to demonstrate these skills will have no problem beginning their career.

—Julia K. Bonafede
PRESIDENT, WILSHIRE CONSULTING
SANTA MONICA, CALIFORNIA

Acknowledgments

To my sister,
Emmelin Northington Golling

Introduction

Finance is the art and science of *making money on money*. This book is about all the ways you can pursue a career doing just that, whether for a few years or a lifetime. There are many ways to work in the finance industry and careers for every type of personality. You do not have to be Warren Buffett or George Soros (though it does not hurt). All you need is drive, determination, and a commitment to the concept of creating wealth from capital. This book will look at some of the most common ways you can do just that.

To begin with let's put investment in its place. It is just one segment of a much greater industry, part of the massive financial services industry, which includes real estate, insurance, commercial banking, corporate finance, and many other disciplines. This book does not pretend to cover all the professions available in that larger arena of finance; instead, it focuses narrowly on investment jobs. Even in this narrow niche, however, the employment market is large and multifaceted. So fasten your seat belts, and prepare to learn about all these possibilities and more.

How to Use This Book

Chapter 1, "Industry History," chronicles the finance industry over the past 5,000 years of human civilization. By any measure it has been a turbulent and exciting ride. Few industries can match this one for sheer drama and magnitude. As one of mankind's oldest professions (perhaps *the* oldest profession), the money trade has been around since ancient Greece. Yet even though cultures and names have changed, much remains the same. Today's hedge fund titans and financial capitalists bear more than a passing resemblance to innovative financiers of the past, like Jacob Fugger, J. P. Morgan, or John Jacob Astor. Equally compelling is the story of how the early stock markets launched the exploration of the North American continent and later helped fuel its growth. History shows that American soil has been fertile ground for financial innovation. Over its short 235-year history the United States has had an unusually high number of pioneering capitalists, each one inventing new ways to "make money on money." Overall the goal of this chapter is to put our present careers in the context of careers past, hoping that the triumphs and travails of historic figures will shed light on ours.

In Chapter 2, "State of the Industry," our perspective changes from past to present. We start out by considering some of the major forces shaping the industry today. Globalism or the growing interconnectedness of capital markets will change the way we buy and sell securities in ways we can hardly imagine today. The financial paradigm is gradually changing, with traditional money centers facing competition from new capital markets in Europe, Asia, and Latin America. Even in the United States the jobs map has become remarkably dispersed over all parts of the country. These trends will have major repercussions for the future job market and should not be overlooked by aspiring professionals.

To understand the future course of specific job titles, we will next look at some hard data from the United States Bureau of Labor Statistics. Its analysis is a good starting point for deciding which careers will be in highest demand from now to the year 2018. We will then examine the regulatory framework of the U.S. securities industry. Beginning with federal regulations, we will review each of the laws passed by the U.S. Congress since 1933. These laws are the cornerstone of all securities regulation in the United States. Understanding their key provisions is mandatory for any aspiring investment professional. We will also look at other regulatory entities, including the National Futures Association, which is the self-regulatory arm of the futures and options industries; the recently formed Financial Industry Regulatory Authority, which issues the licenses needed by most securities professionals; the Municipal Securities Rulemaking Board, which self-regulates the municipal bond market; the North American Securities Administrators Association, a Pan-American voluntary organization founded in 1919; and the International Organization of Securities Commissions, a worldwide organization that may serve as a model for global cooperatives of the future. Finally, Chapter 2 will look at five key sectors in the securities industry, Investment Banking, Securities Brokerage, Venture Capital, Investment Management, and Alternative Investments. These broad sector overviews will set the stage for later chapters that will concentrate on the day-to-day practical side of the business.

Chapter 3, "On the Job," will home in on the details of individual job titles. We will look at 20 different jobs within five functional categories, including financial analysis, trading and brokerage, asset management, advisory services, and government regulation. No matter how interesting or even glamorous a career may appear at a distance, what really matters is how *you personally* will fit into it. With this in mind, we will go on the job and examine its real-life daily activities. We will consider whether they are desk jobs or travel jobs, entry level or experienced only, suitable for self-employment or not.

Often overlooked in career planning is the human factor: whether a particular job is suited for extroverts or introverts, social animals or independent spirits. Some jobs require team players with superior diplomatic and group skills, while others demand an entrepreneurial type who can execute with minimal supervision. With this in mind, our review will consider the people factor. Advancement opportunities are another key consideration. Some jobs are stepping-stones for greater things, while others are career endpoints. Finally, the chapter will briefly examine the credentials needed for a particular role. These are not necessarily mandatory requirements, just recommended skills or experience that may better equip you to compete in today's crowded market.

The investment world is full of money chasers hoping to strike it rich. Without the frenzied chase, it would not be such an exciting field. But eventually one must come down to earth and do a reality check. Chapter 4 takes you through that sometimes-grueling process. Do you *really* want to do investment or do you just want to be rich? Investment is best suited for people who can realistically answer "yes" to both of those questions. Not only should you search your motives, you should search your pocketbook. Do you have sufficient funds to pay the often-steep costs—both in time and education—of entry to the field? Once these issues are put to rest, try putting yourself into the recruiter's shoes, sizing yourself up just as he or she will do. All in all, Chapter 4 puts you through a healthy exercise in self-scrutiny, as well as giving you tools to analyze the costs and benefits of an investment career.

One of the biggest challenges faced by novices is mastering the language of a new vocation. Every industry has its own vernacular, some slang and other terms official enough to be listed in Webster's dictionary. There is also a vast library of technical terms that every professional must master. Our list in Chapter 5, "Talk Like a Pro," serves as a good refresher course in industry terminology, including the jargon, nicknames, and colloquialisms used by insiders every day.

Chapter 6, "Resources," is a compilation of resources for financial professionals. Included is information for job seekers, such as career guides, trade associations, and company directories. These can help you locate names of firms in every sector, do in-depth research on financial companies, and identify networking opportunities. A list of financial magazines and newspapers in both print and online formats is provided, ranging from well-known brand names to niche publications. Also included is an assortment of nonfiction books with financial themes, written by some of the famous names of finance. Their investing philosophies and theories are presented in readable, nonacademic formats.

Most of the career tools have an electronic presence of some sort, and we provide Web links wherever possible. In addition to electronic career guides, we provide links to governmental and regulatory sites, as well as to classic research sources like Hoover's and Moody's. Electronic directories can provide everything from lists of initial public offerings (IPOs) to investment banks to hedge funds. Our educational resources include a list of license test preparation guides, annual ranking providers, and major MBA schools in the United States. Often overlooked as an information resource are museums and archives devoted to finance. We list two of them here.

On a less practical note, we include a list of novels and biographies, some serious and some just for fun. They will not help you get a job, but will hopefully enrich your perspective on the industry you are about to enter. The biographies of legendary figures of finance, from Jay Gould to J. P. Morgan to George Soros, are either inspiring or admonitory but never boring. Also guaranteed to educate and entertain is a list of novels, some classic and some contemporary. The selection includes financial thrillers, murder mysteries, and cautionary tales of all kinds. These are painless ways to learn about finance without ever picking up a textbook. Hollywood's version of Wall Street is put on display in several of the movies we list here, as well as a few "indies" that present the quirky, private view of finance. While you should not expect them to teach you much about the real industry, they are guaranteed to give you plenty to laugh about with your colleagues.

We hope this book serves as a launching pad for your career in the finance industry, giving you both strategic and practical tools for managing your goals. And though investment is a serious business for serious-minded folk, there is a lighter side to it too. So do not forget to have fun with some of those novels and films in your spare time (if you can find any).

Chapter 1

Industry History

In the old days a man who saved money was a miser; nowadays he's a wonder.

—Old Adage

The history of money-making is the history of humanity. Since the dawn of civilization, it has been inextricably linked with human activities. Next to love, it is the great motivator, driving people to extremes to get it and keep it. History shows that money can turn paupers into kings and dregs into tycoons. These dramatic possibilities have made money-making one of the most sought-after professions on earth.

Money was once a bag of coins stuffed in a mattress. Today it is a wisp of electronic energy darting through cyberspace in a fraction of a second. That transformation has taken 6,000 years of human trial and error to achieve. From hoarding to hedge funds, history shows that mankind is infinitely inventive when it comes to money. Here is a capsule overview of the events that created the modern world of investment.

Early Experiments in Securities Trading

In the beginning people hoarded their wealth. Gold, jewels and coins were stockpiled, and the larger the pile, the greater the wealth. Later mankind realized that the pile could be put to more productive use. They discovered that surplus wealth could be lent to rulers, governments, or traders for a fee. Thus the concept of interest or "making money on money" was born.

This was nothing short of a revolution in human thought. Yet the idea of turning a profit from a financial transaction, which involved no "honest" physical labor, was fraught with controversy from its very inception. Even in more sophisticated trading areas like ancient Rome, money lending was viewed as unjust and unnatural. The people who engaged in this dubious trade were viewed with suspicion, which forced them to carry out their transactions under a cloud of moral ambiguity.

These beliefs had originated earlier in Greece during the fourth century B.C.E. Aristotle had developed the concept of a "fair price" for any good or service. According to this worldview, the prices of goods were presumed to be fixed, created by the gods. Man had no right to alter those prices or to seek profits from the fluctuations thereof. The price of a bushel of grain or keg of wine was just as immutable as the laws governing the universe.

Yet money always finds a way. Even the condemnation of the Greek philosophers did not stop money lending from emerging in the early Roman Republic. This was a time of flourishing trade and commerce, both domestic and international. Some traders began to grow wealthy, accumulating excess cash and commodities. Other traders needed to finance the purchase of goods. So those with excess cash on their hands began to extend credit to buyers—for a price. The lenders' willingness to take a risk with their money to turn a profit was a turning point in the history of money.

As the economic power of the early Republic grew, so did the need for large capital. To fuel expansion projects, the Roman government needed to borrow money for road building, land purchase, and street laying. They turned to their provincial tax collectors, the *publicani,* who paid them their taxes in advance (essentially a loan to the government) in exchange for interest. The publicani then used the excess funds to become money lenders, charging interest on loans made to average Roman citizens. The publicani were financially innovative in other ways too. Pooling their wealth—and this could include both coins and commodities like cattle or grain—into a single entity, they created an enterprise for the purpose of limiting individual risk. Similar to a modern day corporation, the new entity (*corpus*) divided ownership into shares of two types: *soccii* (like preferred stock) held by the publicani, and *particulae,* (like common stock) for sale to others.

The Forum in central Rome was the center of trading for these primitive securities. There in the shadow of the great temples, lenders, brokers, and traders congregated to do their deals. The raucous gathering was akin to a loosely organized stock exchange where shares of particulae could be purchased, along with bonds, commodities, cattle, slaves, and land. As in a modern exchange, share values could fluctuate wildly, leading to rampant speculation and the accusation that the Forum was little more than a gambling den. Open to noncitizens, the nascent exchange was a fully international forum where trade deals were transacted and foreign currencies were bought and sold.

Medieval Europe and the Prohibition against Usury

Unfortunately the budding securities market did not survive the fall of Rome. With the rise of Christianity came renewed efforts to throttle any type of economic activity based on interest, credit or the profit motive. In the fourth century c.e. St. Augustine reinvigorated the idea that the pursuit of profit was a sin. The Council of Nicaea had issued a canon in 325 c.e. specifically prohibiting the practice of usury among its clerics. The prohibition was upheld by other Roman Catholic authorities, including Popes Leo the Great and Alexander III, in subsequent centuries. Biblical passages were often quoted as proof that earning interest was a sin against God. One passage in

Fast Facts

A Victorian Woman on Wall Street

When you think of Wall Street tycoons, the name Hetty Green probably does not come to mind. But this 19th-century woman was able to do something that no other woman of her generation could: make a major fortune on Wall Street. Although she made millions betting on greenbacks after the Civil War, she is remembered mostly for her legendary stinginess. Variously called "the Scrooge of Hoboken" or "the Witch of Wall Street," poor Hetty never got much respect. That may be why we remember J. P. Morgan, Daniel Drew, and Jim Fisk, but not Hetty Green.

Deuteronomy 23 was cited as special proof: "Thou shall not lend upon usury to thy brother; usury of money, usury of victuals, usury of anything."

During the reign of Charlemagne in the ninth century, the prohibition was extended to everyone—laymen and clerics alike—by the Capitularies of Charlemagne. Thus for the first time in history, the concept of interest was under attack by both church and state. In the 11th century, perhaps in response to the revival of European trade, the attack by civil and religious authorities intensified. Usury was declared a form of theft and a violation of the Seventh Commandment, the consequence of which was excommunication or imprisonment.

The effect on medieval trade and commerce was chilling, but it did not stop money lending altogether. Merchants and bankers went to great lengths to carry out their commercial activities while circumventing the prohibition in a sort of "loophole" that will be familiar to people today. They justified their profits by claiming they were exempt from the usury edict because they were charging a "fair price," as defined by Aristotle in earlier centuries. Or they claimed that money lending was just and fair because they were helping out a poor debtor. In essence these early capitalists were spin masters of great skill who cloaked their actions in piety as a way of evading civil and religious authorities.

The Financial Revolution of the Renaissance

Despite the official condemnation of usury in medieval Europe, certain classes of money lenders emerged anyway. In Italian trading cities like Venice, Siena, and Genoa, new types of capitalists surfaced from groups that were marginal to mainstream society. Among them were Lombards and Jews. Originally a Germanic tribe, the pagan Lombards settled in the Kingdom of Genoa, but resisted efforts to convert to Christianity and did not assimilate into society. Yet their marginal social status freed them to innovate financially in ways that Christians never could. Likewise, Jews gravitated toward money lending because they were excluded from mainstream professions and were not subject to the Christian Church's prohibition against usury. These groups formed the basis of the Italian merchant bankers. A Jewish money lender, Shylock, was fictionalized in Shakespeare's 1598 play, *The Merchant of Venice*. Because Shylock is depicted as a ruthless exploiter of debtors, demanding "a pound of flesh" as security for the loan, his name has become synonymous with *loan shark*. The caricature shows how money lending was continuing to be viewed with disdain, even in 16th century England.

One man did not see the contradiction between Christianity and money lending. Bavarian merchant banker Jacob Fugger (1459–1526) was both a devout Catholic and one of the earliest men to amass a colossal fortune by "making money on money." His grandfather, Hans Fugger, had started out by trading in commodities; gradually, over time, the family accumulated excess cash and started trading in money instead. Jacob, the greatest financier of his family, lent money to monarchs and popes for interest. He also mobilized private capital from multiple investors to finance his enterprises, thus becoming one of the earliest merchant bankers in Europe. Earlier wealthy men had been rulers, conquerors or popes; Jacob Fugger proved that an average person could become a millionaire. Upon his death, he was worth the equivalent of $75 million in today's dollars.

The Origins of European Stock Markets

In the mid- to late-medieval period, trade and commerce expanded, towns prospered, and a middle class emerged. These economic transformations gradually led to a loosening of restrictions on money lending and profit. The greatest seedbed of financial innovation in this period was in the city-states of what is now Italy. Trading towns like Florence, Venice, Genoa, and Milan were evolving into truly modern cities. Money lending and foreign currency exchange were key financial activities, as was trading in government bonds. At first moneylenders traded debt only between themselves; later, they sold debt to outsiders, thereby creating an "investor" class. Neither debtor nor creditor with no direct interest in the transaction, this new type of financier had only one interest in the deal: *profit*. Italian bankers were also gradually expanding their operations to "satellite" locations like London, where they served as creditors to the English.

Similar financial innovations arose in northern Europe. In France, the *courratiers de change* managed the debts of agricultural communities and also traded the debt. Functioning as brokers, these people met in an established place to ply their trades. Flemish towns like Bruges, Antwerp, and Ghent were also centers of commerce and trade. A stock exchange had developed in Bruges by 1531, though it did not actually trade stocks per se—only bonds. Meeting in a building owned by the Van der Beurze family, the assemblage of brokers came to be known as the *Beurze*, a term that quickly spread to other towns. Over the centuries *Beurze* would transform into *Börze* in German and *Bourse* in French, both modern words for "stock exchange."

Financing Global Exploration

The age of global exploration provided a treasure trove of money-making opportunities for merchant bankers of the day. These adventurous investors were early incarnations of today's venture capitalists. Trading with Asia was enormously risky in those days. Pirate attacks, storms, and shipwrecks were constant threats. To lessen the risks of losing cargo, ship owners would seek out investors to underwrite the expeditions. In return for their risk, they were promised a hefty share of the profits. The vehicle used for the transaction was an early form of the limited liability company, which spread the risks among multiple investors. One of the first enterprises was the Muscovy Company, which financed the search for the Northwest Passage. Chartered by the English Crown in 1531 for trade with Russia, it became England's first joint stock company.

Even more noteworthy was the famed Dutch East India Company, a joint stock company formed in 1602 to finance trade with Asia. It would produce average dividends of 18 percent for its investors during its nearly 200 years of existence. It was the first company to issue shares on the newly formed Amsterdam Stock Exchange. As the most sophisticated stock exchange in Europe at the time, the Amsterdam Exchange would become a major financing arm for global exploration. Shares were issued on paper, which could then be sold to other investors: a truly novel idea for the times. The exchange also pioneered in many financial techniques (short selling, debt-equity swaps, unit trusts, options trading) still familiar to us.

Also traded on the Amsterdam Exchange was the Dutch West India Company, formed for the purpose of financing the exploration of North America. The company backed the settlement of Manhattan in the mid-17th century, and its influence on the financial industry of New York would reverberate for centuries thereafter. In addition to the Dutch, the English were key investors in the exploration of North America. The London Virginia Company would finance the settlement of Virginia and other southern colonies. Individual merchant adventurers also helped underwrite the colonization and settlement of the New World.

The Modern Market Emerges

The earliest securities trading in London was carried out by the Lombardi and Jewish Italian immigrants who had settled there in the early medieval period. Early trading was in the streets, but by 1567 it had become formal enough to open an indoor exchange. Called the Royal Exchange, it was a clearinghouse for commercial paper and was also a place where brokers would gossip, idle, and cavort. These traders were known for their rowdy behavior; one group of brokers was so unruly that it was banned from the Exchange. Undeterred, they simply moved their trading to the local coffeehouses. Thus, the surrounding neighborhood became known as "Exchange Alley" where coffeehouses (Lloyds, Jonathan's, and Galloway's) catering to money men sprung up. These were much more than places to partake of the strong brew—they amounted to stock exchanges in themselves, where deals were struck, money changed hands, and fortunes were won and lost. In fact, money and coffee became so closely intertwined that Jonathan's Coffeehouse was renamed "The Stock Exchange" in 1773. Twenty-eight years later, the former coffeehouse became an "official" trading institution when its members reorganized as a joint stock company, now calling itself the London Stock Exchange.

The American Experiment

As British subjects, the thirteen American colonies did not have a formal stock market, but instead relied upon the English financial system for growth and development. Under English law, the colonists' economic and investment activities were severely restricted. They were required under terms of the Navigation Acts of 1663–1712 to import all their manufactured goods from England, at whatever price English middlemen wanted them to pay. This, of course, lined the pockets of English merchants and agents to the detriment of colonial buyers. Likewise for most of the colonial era, the settlers were restricted to the English market for exports of their agricultural and forest products. The development of capital markets was further hampered by the colonies' heavy reliance on barter and credit as a means of exchange. As a result of these and other economic restrictions, capital markets failed to emerge in the pre-Revolutionary era. Not surprisingly this became a source of the unrest that drove the revolt against Great Britain.

Even without an established institution, some informal trading did take place in colonial coffeehouses. By 1754 colonists were

Everyone Knows

Origin of the Term "Blue Sky Laws"

Blue Sky Laws protect investors from fraudulent schemes. First passed by the Kansas legislature in 1911, the laws require securities firms to file a description of their operations, get a permit, and register their brokers. The term "blue sky" probably originated when a Kansas bank commissioner rallied against fraudulent investments, claiming they were "backed by nothing but the blue skies of Kansas." The term was later picked up by newspapers, who called them "blue sky laws."

trading bonds at the London Coffeehouse in Philadelphia. This legendary establishment was a seedbed of revolutionary ideas: so much so that the British promptly closed it down. Undeterred, the rebel-financiers simply moved their trading activities down the street to another watering hole, the City Tavern. Yet even up to the eve of the Revolution, the colonies had no organized venue for securities trading. The growing conflict forced them to invent one, and fast. Philadelphia led the way, opening the young nation's first formal stock exchange—the Philadelphia Board of Brokers—in 1790.

New York City was not far behind. Its stock exchange also arose out of a café: Tontine's Coffeehouse in lower Manhattan. Thus began a ferocious rivalry between Philadelphia and New York, each vying for the title of financial capital of the young nation. New York decided that the best way to compete was to formalize its trading practices. At the time trading had become so lax that it had moved outdoors to the curbs, functioning more like a street fair than a financial organization. Fraud and trade rigging were widespread. To combat these problems, two dozen brokers met in 1792 under a buttonwood tree at 68 Wall Street. They reached an agreement on acceptable trading practices, including setting a fixed commission. Called the Buttonwood Agreement, this was the earliest incarnation of the New York Stock Exchange. However, brokers were unwilling to give up their coffeehouses: they continued to trade in the caffeinated venues for two more decades.

The Origins of Wall Street and Merchant Banking

After the war of independence the Buttonwood members began trading in government war bonds and issuing stocks in new enterprises. Its first "IPO" was the Bank of New York, followed by issues of other banks. Some traders, however, continued to meet on the curb, even in the dead of winter. This group came to be known as "The Curb Exchange," a name it retained until the 1950s when it was renamed The American Stock Exchange (AMEX). For their part, the Buttonwood traders continued to formalize, adopting a constitution and code of conduct, as well as setting listing requirements and fee structures. By 1817, with just 30 listings, it was meeting in a rented room at 40 Wall Street and calling itself The New York Stock and Exchange Board. Cost of a membership seat was $25.

Yet public stock was not sufficient to finance a rapidly growing nation in the early 19th century. Much larger capital resources were needed to expand westward and develop the nation's industrial infrastructure: railroads, telegraph, and roads. These economic pressures triggered an important development in the history of American finance: the rise of the investment banking company. Two of the first were Nicholas Biddle and Company of Philadelphia and Prime, Ward and King in New York City. The Rothschild family, at the time the most powerful private bankers in the world, also set up merchant banking operations in the United States during this period.

Fueled by wars and political turmoil, the young nation was plagued by wide swings in its economy. Some shrewd entrepreneurs exploited the ups and downs to their advantage. One of them was John Jacob Astor, a German immigrant who built a fortune in land speculation and commodity trading. He earned an effective return of 100 percent on his investment in the risky and depreciated U.S. government bonds that underwrote the War of 1812. The second was Stephen Girard, a Philadelphia banker who turned a huge profit by buying out the beleaguered stocks of American banks and companies. In both cases, huge fortunes were made by taking equally huge risks with downtrodden securities.

The Age of Global Stock Markets

Across the globe in the 18th and 19th centuries, stock markets grew in size and stature. In Europe, loosely organized medieval exchanges began to formalize and take on their modern forms. Vienna's stock

INTERVIEW

How the Industry's Past Is Shaping Its Future

A. R. (Rob) Hoxton IV, CFP(r), AIF(r)
CEO & Senior Wealth Advisor, Hoxton Financial, Inc.
(Interview conducted with a staff member of Hoxton Financial, Inc.)

Please describe Rob's professional experience in the finance industry, including the number of years he has worked in it.
Rob began his career in financial services while in college, working first in an insurance agency. After graduation he joined American International Group (AIG) in New York and later left to establish Hoxton Financial, Inc., a fee-only registered investment advisor and financial planning firm based in his home town of Shepherdstown, West Virginia. Since entering the financial services industry over 20 years ago, Hoxton has built a reputation as a financial planner, investment manager, author, and industry leader. In addition to operating Hoxton Financial, he serves on the national board of directors of The Financial Planning Association, and is the founder of The Rural Financial Planning Project, a volunteer organization which promotes financial planning as a career choice for rural students in Appalachia (www.ruralplanner.com).

How has working in the investments services industry changed since he started working in it? What is today's investment professional facing that past professionals did not face?
When Rob entered the industry over 20 years ago, he was hired as an insurance agent. As was the case for most new entrants, initial professional education focused almost entirely on sales skills and the level of sales activity that would make a new "advisor" successful. The customary practice prior to hire was to have the advisor candidate develop a list of contacts who could later be prospected and solicited for business. In his company the exercise was called "Project 100". Stories of similar sales cultures in other organizations have been popularized in movies like *The Pursuit of Happyness*, starring Will Smith. Historically, the industry has focused primarily on sales training and business building attributes instead of professional education and training. Interestingly, despite the industry's focus on sales skills, the failure rate remained alarmingly high. Only once the new advisor had clawed his/her way to success would he/she begin to pursue substantive professional education such as the Certified Financial Planner(r) professional designation. Sadly, without sufficient supervision, the new advisor could well do more harm than good to a trusting client's financial well-being.

The recent proliferation of financial planning curricula at universities such as Shepherd University, Texas Tech, Boston University, and Virginia Tech now puts education ahead of sales skills. Now new college graduates have the building blocks for a successful career and are ready to join investment firms armed for success, both for themselves and for the client. Sales and business development skills are just as important as ever but now more than ever, wealth management firms have created a safe environment for the new advisor to learn the business, participate in a structure apprenticeship and emerge as someone who adds value not only for his/her employer but also the client.

New challenges abound. With passage of the Dodd-Frank Act in 2010, financial representatives who provide custom advice to consumers will be held to a fiduciary standard of care when working with those clients. The fiduciary standard of care stands in stark contrast to the traditional sales model in which advisors are only required to abide by suitability standards when selling financial products and investments. The brokerage community continues to fight this legal development, preferring instead to operate sales organizations while simultaneously holding themselves out as client-centric financial advisors. The result of this development, while favorable to the end consumer, may erect barriers for new advisors who do not have an educational foundation in financial topics such as investments, insurance, tax, and employee benefits.

How have educational and professional training requirements changed in the past few decades?
Though educational and professional training requirements have not changed much in the past few decades, consumers have begun to demand that advisors be more than just great sales people. In response to this demand, a multitude of organizations have emerged to provide credentials for advisors. Many of these organizations offer little more than the opportunity for advisors to buy credentials. That being said, a handful of credentialing entities such as The CFP(r) Board of Standards (Certified Financial Planner), The Center for Fiduciary Studies (Accredited Investment Fiduciary) and The CFA Institute (Chartered Financial Analyst) provide both a rigorous course of study and ongoing educational requirement of professional who have been licensed to use their designations.

In further response to this trend, universities from around the country have added financial planning curriculum for interested students. Graduates of these degree programs will be the future leaders of the financial services profession.

(continued on next page)

INTERVIEW

How the Industry's Past Is Shaping Its Future
(continued)

What are some of the most significant events (the ones that shaped it the most) in the past 50 years of the finance industry?

Three events come to mind as the most significant over the past 50 years. To be sure, Rob's career has not spanned the entire 50-year period. He offers one academic event, one market event, and one regulatory event.

Academic: In the hallowed halls of 1950s academia, specifically The University of Chicago, a new, radical way of thinking about investing began to gain traction. Mathematician/statistician Harry Markowitz (it is rumored) was waiting to present his doctoral thesis when he was approached by a stockbroker who challenged him for help with problems that his clients were encountering in the stock market. The result was Markowitz's seminal paper entitled "Portfolio Selection" (The Journal of Finance, 1952). The paper became the foundation of Modern Portfolio Theory and later won him the Nobel Prize in 1990.

Market: The 2008-2009 credit crisis changed not only the way investment managers build and manage portfolios but also pushed the world to the brink of economic disaster. Not since the Great Depression had the world been pushed to the brink. Investment advisors around the world witnessed perfect correlation of virtually all asset classes as values plummeted, sending investors to the relative safety of government bonds. The crisis ushered in a period of new and sweeping financial regulation.

Regulatory: The credit crisis exposed massive fraud amongst investment advisors. Criminal behavior from advisors like Bernard Madoff

exchange was founded in 1771 and would be Eastern Europe's primary capital market until World War II. The Berlin Börse came along in 1817, followed in 1828 by the Australia Stock Market, which opened with just one stock listing. Seventeen years later the Brazil Stock Exchange opened in Rio de Janeiro. As in New York and London, securities trading in Mexico City began on the sidewalks. Other world cities, like Johannesburg, Tokyo, Osaka, Cairo, and Allen Stanford made it clear to Washington that further regulation and oversight is necessary. The Dodd-Frank Act which passed both houses of Congress and was signed into law by the President in 2010 promised to transform the industry in ways not seen since passage of the Investment Advisors Act in 1934.

What are some of the most significant trends in the past 50 years of the finance industry?

The rise of independent investment firms, both broker/dealers and fee-only advice firms has and continues to re-shuffle the landscape of the industry. No longer must financial advisors be affiliated with behemoth investment banks. Technological advances and consumer demands have made the independent firm model viable.

The push for greater transparency and fiduciary care, both from consumers and Washington, will shape the industry for years to come. Despite efforts from Wall Street firms to defeat the fiduciary movement, consumers and politicians are embracing it. Rob is confident that whether or not Dodd-Frank is implemented in its current form, "the horse has left the barn" and the tendency for investors to hold their advisors to a fiduciary standard of care will continue to bend the industry into compliance.

How has the role of women in the investment profession changed over the course of the past half century?

The role of women in the profession has not changed enough. Anecdotally, Rob cites his observation that he still sees a miniscule number of women at industry functions. In his own firm, he is proud to report that more than half of the firm's advisor professionals are women. The career characteristics as reported in a 2009 CNN Money poll should be attractive to men and women alike. Income, lifestyle and client interaction attributes are some of the most attractive of all career fields polled. That being said, Rob states that a larger percentage of students enrolled in university programs are women when compared to the workforce currently deployed.

Medellin, Valparaiso, Santiago, and Alexandria would not organize formal stock exchanges until the late 19th and early 20th centuries.

By the late 19th century the United States had many regional stock exchanges. In addition to Philadelphia and New York, the Boston Stock Exchange (BSE) had opened by 1834. The San Francisco Stock and Bond Exchange opened in 1882 and The Los Angeles Oil Exchange in 1889; the two would merge in 1957 to become the

Pacific Stock Exchange (PSX). Chicago's growth as a Midwest industrial center fueled the opening of an exchange in 1882 (CHX).

Rice, Butter, and Eggs

Commodities exchanges are markets where raw or primary products are bought and sold in standardized contracts. Although they date from the earliest days of civilization, the first organized commodities exchange was probably the Dojima Rice Exchange, founded in 1710 in Osaka, Japan. Chicago would become the location of the United States's first commodities exchange when the Chicago Board of Trade opened in 1848. Its famous trading pit was immortalized in *The Pit,* a 1903 novel by Chicago author Frank Norris.

Futures contracts were invented to address the problem of commodity shortages and gluts that led to erratic price fluctuations. To protect themselves from the risk of adverse price movements, traders developed "cash forward" or futures contracts. The first of these contracts was issued by the Chicago Board of Trade in 1865. In 1898 another landmark event occurred in the Windy City when the Chicago Butter and Egg Board, later called the Chicago Mercantile Exchange, opened up as a nonprofit organization. Today it trades derivatives, futures, and options contracts and has merged with the Chicago Board of Trade to form a single exchange owned by the CME Group.

New York City opened its own commodities exchange in 1872. Here also a group of dairy merchants joined forces and created the Butter and Cheese Exchange of New York. Gradually, more food products were added, including eggs, dried fruit, and poultry. Rather than continuing to add new foods to its title, it settled on the name "New York Mercantile Exchange" a decade later. This organization was the forerunner of NYMEX, now part of the CME Group. Today, CME Group is comprised of four major commodities exchanges: NYMEX, the Commodity Exchange (also known as COMEX), and the previously noted Chicago Mercantile Exchange and Chicago Board of Trade. The official name of the exchanges is Designated Contracts Markets, but in practice, few people use that humdrum title. The former butter and cheese exchange is today a part of a massive global conglomerate that counts a controlling share in the Dow Jones Index among its many holdings—an astonishing metamorphosis indeed.

Fast Facts

Old Wine in New Bottles

The investment term "derivative" came into common usage in the 1970s, referring to a variety of alternative, exotic investments. Yet it is not really a new concept: just an old idea repackaged and reinvented. A derivative is a financial instrument with a value based on a projection of future price movements of its underlying asset. The term refers to the futures and options markets as a whole, including things like rice futures that have been around since the 18th century. What are new are the many types of derivatives now available: swaps, forwards, hybrid securities, and securitized debt (including the infamous subprime mortgage).

The Gilded Age of Investing

In the late 19th century the young nation was growing rapidly. Its need for large pools of capital led to the emergence of risk-taking financiers who would become staggeringly wealthy by investing in new ventures. This was the era of dynamic growth in industry and transportation, especially railroads. It was also the age of American inventiveness. There was money to be made in underwriting the seminal inventions of the times: telephone, telegraph, light bulb, typewriter, phonograph, trolley car, linotype, mimeograph, still camera, motion picture camera, bicycle, automobile, airplane: the list goes on and on. Many of these inventions were backed by private investors like Henry Ford, who founded the Ford Motor Company as a private enterprise. Indeed, the age was rich in venture capital opportunities for those with vision and financial wherewithal.

Making money in this era, often called the Gilded Age, was facilitated by the lack of government regulation of the public stock markets. This was the age of the Wall Street tycoons: larger-than-life figures who dominated the world of investment and made huge fortunes. They were powerful enough to move the markets and often did. Without rules to govern investment activities, a small group of men were able to manipulate the stock markets to their own

advantage. Jay Gould, Daniel Drew, August Belmont, and Corne-
lius Vanderbilt were among them. But as the stock markets crashed
and panics set in (as occurred several times in the late 19th century),
these men were also blamed by an outraged public for its losses.
Investment could also be a deadly business: legendary tycoon and
market mover Jim ("Diamond Jim") Fisk was shot and killed by an
investor and former business associate (who just happened to be the
boyfriend of Fisk's ex-mistress).

The Early 20th Century: Innovation and Turbulence

The turn of the 20th century was a time of rapid innovation. In 1896
The Wall Street Journal introduced the Dow Jones Industrial Average (DJIA). It tracked a mere dozen stocks in such industries as railroad, sugar refining, tobacco, cattle feed, gas, and cotton oil. One
familiar name was among them: General Electric. It is the only company from the original listing still on the DJIA today. Wall Street was
also upgrading its image in those years: In 1903 the NYSE moved its
operations to 18 Broad Street, into a Greek Classical Revival building
with a lofty colonnade and imposing facade. It had come a long way
since its rowdy coffeehouse days.

A new crop of tycoons dominated the investment scene in the
early years of the century, including J. P. Morgan, Jacob Schiff, and
E. H. Harriman. Like their predecessors, they benefited from a largely
unregulated industry, making massive fortunes by monopolizing
segments of the market (an accusation they strenuously denied). Not
surprisingly the times were pockmarked by speculations, panics,
and bank runs, most notably in 1907 when the collapse of the Knickerbocker Trust Company triggered a major run. As suspicions arose
that a small group of financiers were causing or at least benefitting
from these crises, the U.S. Congress stepped in, creating the Federal
Reserve System in 1913. Its purpose was to provide a safety net for
banks, but its effect on Wall Street was to close the loopholes that had
allowed a small cartel of moneyed men to profit from economic collapse. Thus the party had come to an end for the powerful and flam-
boyant merchant princes of the Gilded Age, and investment would
never be the same again.

The average Wall Street investor was changing. By the end of World
War I investors were no longer just the privileged few. Middle class
citizens were now buying stocks. Bonds had long been the favored
investment for average folk, but in the giddy investment climate of

the Roaring Twenties, equity was becoming more popular. Speculating and buying on margin became widespread, even among conservative investors. Efforts by the neophyte Federal Reserve Bank to curtail the "irrational exuberance" did little good. The DJIA hit its peak of 381.17 in September, 1929. The end came on October 24, 1929, when the overleveraged stock market collapsed.

The Rise of Regulated Markets

The lessons learned from the 1929 stock market crash changed the way Wall Street did business. In the aftermath, the U.S. Congress passed two laws to protect investors, the Securities Act of 1933, and a year later, the Securities Exchange Act, which created the Securities and Exchange Commission (SEC). This federal agency's function as to enforce these two laws, as well as legislation passed in later years; i.e., the Trust Indenture Act of 1939, the Investment Advisers Act of 1940, the Investment Company Act of 1940, and the Sarbanes-Oxley Act of 2002. These laws form the core of the federal regulations governing the finance industry today.

The Banking Act of 1933, often called the Glass-Steagall Act, was another major law passed in the wake of the 1929 stock market crash. Although it mainly dealt with the commercial banking industry, one provision had a marked impact on investment practices. It mandated the separation of the commercial and investment banking industries, effectively putting up a "Chinese wall" between the two. This remained the law until 1999 when it was partially dismantled by the Gramm-Leach-Bliley Act, which lifted the provision barring bank holding companies from owning other types of financial firms. The repeal meant that commercial banks, investment banks, securities firms, and even insurance companies could consolidate under one corporate umbrella.

"The Stock Market for the Next Hundred Years"

Another regulatory milestone occurred right before the Second World War. In 1939 the National Association of Securities Dealers (NASD) was established as a self-regulatory authority for the stock markets. It grew out of an amendment to the Securities Exchange Act, the Maloney Act, which gave the NASD authority to supervise the activities of its members. This put the trading of brokers and brokerage firms under the suzerainty of the NASD. Its most famous invention came about in 1971 with the opening of the National Association of Securities Dealers Automated Quotations (NASDAQ), which was the world's first automated exchange. With no physical trading floor, all stocks were traded through a network of mainframe computers. The listings were referred to as "over the counter," or OTC, stocks by the public and media. Its automated trading system reduced the spread between the bid price and ask price of the stock: something that displeased brokers, since it reduced their commissions.

In more ways than one, NASDAQ was an innovative force in the finance industry. It was the first exchange to advertise to the public with its well-known slogan, "The stock market for the next hundred years." The slogan was certainly accurate when it came to computerized trading systems, which, of course, have become the industry standard. With its relaxed listing requirements, NASDAQ became the market for newly formed or small companies that could not meet the stricter requirements of the NYSE and AMEX.

But that was all in the future. The First World War marked a turning point in American financial history. The United States was now a creditor rather than a debtor nation and was the creditor of Europe in the war's aftermath. Wall Street had finally surpassed Lombard Street (the historical location of London's banks and investment houses) as the financial center of the world.

A New Day Dawns on Wall Street

Other things on Wall Street were also changing. While the men were away at war in 1943, women were admitted to the trading floor of the NYSE for the first time. Their presence on the trading floor was a major milestone, though they were still not allowed to buy membership seats. That did not occur until 1967 when 35-year-old Muriel Siebert made history as the first female member of the NYSE: the only woman in a club of 1,365 men. In 1975 after the NYSE relaxed its rules on the negotiation of commissions, Muriel Siebert and Company was the first to announce its new status as a discount brokerage house. She continued to make financial history when she became New York State's first female Superintendent of Banks in 1977.

A lesser-known Wall Street pioneer is Joseph Searles, who in 1970 became the first African-American member of the NYSE. He worked at the now-defunct Wall Street firm of Newberger, Loeb & Company. According to *In the Black: A History of African-Americans on Wall Street* by Gregory S. Bell, Searles faced a mixed reception at best from his fellow members. "Some members were very helpful, and then others, I could see beneath their smiles that they wanted to cut my guts," Searles recalls. "It was a time of change in America and most of the younger generation were [sic] accepting change more gracefully than their fathers."

The difficult position of minorities and women on Wall Street is suggested by the situation they encountered at the Stock Exchange Luncheon Club, an exclusive, members-only dining club located a few floors above the trading floor. Founded in 1898, the club's dining room was known for its plush design. It was decorated with stuffed animal heads, supposedly acquired by its members on African safaris. But it had no ladies restroom until 1987, two decades after a woman was first admitted as a member. Searles, for his part, had to eat at a table by himself, at least for a while. According to Bell, the new member did not exactly get the red carpet treatment. "At the time, my biggest fear...was where would I sit in the luncheon club? We didn't want to upset or offend members of the NYSE luncheon club."

The legendary club finally closed in 2006, for reasons that might best be explained by author P. J. O'Rourke. In his 1999 book, *Eat the Rich: A Treatise on Economics*, he describes the club as follows: "The ceilings are lofty, the windows are Palladian, and the help is obsequious. The leather armchairs are wide and deep. The china is monogrammed. The stalls in the men's room are made of marble. And all day long, the New York Stock Exchange Luncheon Club is empty... The traders gobble take-out food, standing up."

Discount Brokerages and Electronic Trading

Muriel Siebert's firm was only one of several brokerages that rushed to take advantage of the deregulation of stock trading commissions when the announcement came in 1975. Up to that time, commission structures had always been fixed, not only in the United States but also in London, Canada, Australia, and Japan. Members of traditional stock exchanges dealt with one another on a preferential basis and prohibited nonmembers from entering the trading floor. The SEC's statement came on May 1, 1975 (often called Wall Street's "May Day"). It precipitated nothing short of a revolution in the finance industry. Charles Schwab, a California company in existence since 1973, announced its intention to become a discount brokerage, as did other firms. These brokerages offered lower fees and commissions in exchange for customers doing their own research and reaching investment decisions on their own. Once the United States had taken this quantum leap, other exchanges faced competitive pressures to do likewise. England, Canada, and Australia followed by deregulating their commission structures in the 1980s; Japan, however, did not deregulate until 1997.

The abolition of fixed commission rates led to other industry changes. Many securities firms incorporated and became public companies, eventually transforming themselves into financial conglomerates. In the early 1990s many global stock exchanges also became public corporations. The advent of fully electronic communications networks was also making the traditional trading floor increasingly irrelevant.

Options Go Mainstream

No one know for sure when options trading first developed, but variants of it were around in ancient Rome, Greece, and Phoenicia. Options were used by the Dutch to trade tulips in the 17th century and in England a century later. Yet they were very controversial: people lost money so often that they were eventually banned in several countries. In the United States, a type of option first appeared in the early 19th century, but it was not traded on any exchange. Instead sellers typically placed ads in the newspaper to find buyers. Due to the illiquidity of the market, options trading was a marginal investment activity at best, and growth in volume was slow. Corruption and fraud were widespread and went mostly unchecked. In the early 1900s options trading became a bit more respectable with the development of an over-the-counter market. Yet even then the market remained small, encumbered by a lack of market information and complicated rules.

In the 1970s the Chicago Board of Trade took steps to address these problems. Its solution was a new exchange that standardized the rules; instituted a system of market makers; and created a clearinghouse, Options Clearing Corporation, to issue contracts and guarantee settlement. By 1973 the Chicago Board Options Exchange (CBOE) was open for trading, initially listing 16 call options. Several years later trading in put options began after the SEC approved the practice. They become especially popular after financial newspapers began printing options prices, and when other exchanges like PSX and AMEX began listing them. Options trading volume rose sharply; by the end of 1974, average daily volume had topped 200,000.

Another pivotal event in the history of options occurred in 1973. In that year two obscure academics, Myron Scholes and Fischer Black, published an academic paper outlining a new options pricing model. Called the Black-Scholes Model, its purpose was to determine a fair market value for call options. Its larger impact on the industry was to reduce the perceived risk of options trading, thereby encouraging more and more people to get into options.

The 1980s and 1990s saw explosive growth in options trading. What had once been limited to an elite club of insiders was now a mass-market phenomenon. Further tools were developed to track the market, such as the CBOE Volatility Index, which tracked volatility in real time. The 1987 stock market crash temporarily dampened the market's enthusiasm for options, but it recovered its volumes in the next decade. By 1999, open contract volume had eclipsed 60 million. Today five exchanges are involved in United States options trading, including the most recent entrant, the International Securities Exchange (ISE), which opened in 2000.

Mergers, Acquisitions, and Name Changes

One of the most confusing things about the finance industry is that so many entities and organizations have changed their names. Usually this occurs through mergers and acquisitions. NASDAQ's story is especially complicated, a veritable alphabet soup of name changes. In 1996 it was accused by the SEC of putting its interests as the operator of NASDAQ ahead of its responsibilities as a regulator. As a result, the organization was split in two parts, one entity regulating the brokers and brokerage firms, and the other regulating the NASDAQ stock market. However, additional changes occurred in 2007 when the NASD merged with the NYSE. When this happened, the regulatory arm of NASDAQ was renamed the Financial Institution Regulatory Authority (FINRA). Today, FINRA is the self-regulatory authority that governs the activities of brokers and brokerage firms.

NASDAQ also merged with a few other exchanges. In 1998 it merged with the American Stock Exchange, and by the start of the 21st century the combined entity was the largest electronic stock market in the United States. In 2007 NASDAQ acquired the Philadelphia Stock Exchange, which is now known as NASDAQ OMX PHLX. This merger united the country's oldest stock exchange with the futuristic exchange "for the next hundred years." And finally, in 2008, NASDAQ acquired the Boston Stock Exchange, now known as NASDAQ OMX BX.

The pace of industry change speeded up dramatically in the last years of the 20th century. In the next chapter, we will examine these recent events and how they created the finance industry we know today.

A Brief Chronology

Fourth century B.C.E.: Aristotle establishes concept of "fair price."

Second century B.C.E.: Early Roman experiment in stock exchange and securities.

325 C.E.: Council of Nicaea prohibits usury among clerics.

Ninth century C.E.: Capitularies of Charlemagne extends usury prohibition to all Christians, both clerics and laymen alike.

1475-1523: Life of Jacob Fugger, merchant banking pioneer.

1598: William Shakespeare publishes *The Merchant of Venice*, a play about an Italian merchant and a Jewish moneylender.

1531: Founding of Belgian stock exchange. Founding of the Muscovy Company.

1567: The Royal Exchange trades indoors for first time.

1602: Founding of the entity that would become the Amsterdam Stock Exchange (Amsterdam Bourse). The Dutch East India is the first company to list on the Amsterdam Stock Exchange.

1653: A wall is built across lower Manhattan island to protect Dutch settlers from attack by the British and Native Americans.

1685: A street is laid out along a walking path behind the old Dutch wall by city planners. The walking path becomes Wall Street. The Berlin Stock Exchange (Berliner Börse) is founded.

1710: First known commodities exchange opens in Osaka, Japan.

1724: Louis XV officially recognizes the Paris Stock Exchange (Paris Bourse).

1771: Vienna Stock Market (Wiener Börse) founded in Vienna, Austria.

1773: Jonathan's Coffeehouse in London is renamed "The Stock Exchange."

1775: American Manufactory of Woolens, Linens and Cottons is first American industrial company traded on a stock exchange.

1790: Federal government issues bonds to finance Revolutionary War debt, thus inaugurating beginnings of U.S. investment markets. Philadelphia Board of Brokers established.

1792: Twenty-four bankers sign Buttonwood Agreement, a forerunner to the New York Stock Exchange.

1793: Tontine's Coffeehouse, an informal trading exchange, opens in lower Manhattan.

1799: Demise of Dutch East India Company after almost 200 years of existence.

1801: The Stock Exchange is renamed The London Stock Exchange.

1803: Louisiana Purchase financed by UK investment firm, Barings.

1815: First published stock table appears in *New York Commercial Advertiser.*

1817: Buttonwood brokers establish New York Stock and Exchange Board and rents space at 40 Wall Street. The Berlin Börse is founded.

1826: Investment bank Prime, Ward & King founded in New York City.

1827: Baltimore & Ohio Railroad listed on New York exchange.

1828: Australia's first stock exchange opens in Sydney with just one stock.

1834: Boston Stock Exchange opens.

1845: Rio de Janeiro Stock Exchange (Bolsa de Valores do Rio de Janeiro) founded in Rio de Janeiro, Brazil.

1848: Chicago Board of Trade established.

1853: NYSE issues first disclosure requirements.

1865: The NYSE moves into its permanent home at 10-12 Broad Street, south of Wall Street.

1867: Stock ticker invented by Edward Calahan.

1868: NYSE members allowed to buy and sell seats.

1869: NYSE requires all shares of listed companies to be registered at banks.

1874: Chicago Produce Exchange established (forerunner of Chicago Mercantile Exchange).

1878: Stock exchanges founded in Tokyo and Osaka, Japan.

1882: San Francisco Stock and Bond Exchange opens for business. Chicago opens its first stock market.

1884: Charles Dow devises an average of stock prices of a dozen leading companies and publishes it in his daily newspaper.

1889: The Johannesburg Stock Exchange is founded in South Africa. *Customer's Afternoon Letter*, published by Charles Dow and Edward

Jones, later renamed the *Wall Street Journal*. The Los Angeles Oil Exchange opens.

1896: *Wall Street Journal* introduces Dow Jones Industrial Average.

1898: Chicago Butter and Egg Board opens as nonprofit organization.

1900: John Moody publishes first bond ratings.

1903: A stock exchange opens in Cairo, Egypt. Frank Norris publishes *The Pit*, a novel that immortalizes the trading pit at the Chicago Board of Trade. NYSE moves to 18 Broad Street.

1907: Panic of 1907 ensues with failure of Knickerbocker Trust Company.

1911: Kansas adopts "blue sky" laws, leading to passage of similar laws in 22 other states.

1913: Federal Reserve System is established to bring stability to investment and banking industry.

1914: NYSE closes for 14 months over fears of capital flight resulting from threat of war in Europe.

1915: Charles Lynch and Peter Merrill found brokerage company.

1921: New York Curb Exchange moves indoors; will eventually become American Stock Exchange.

1924: Massachusetts Investors Trust and State Street Investment Trust are founded; becomes first mutual funds.

1929: Scudder issues first no-load funds.

1929: Stock market crashes on October 24th.

1933: The Banking Act of 1933 (the Glass-Steagall Act) creates "Chinese wall" between investment and banking activities at financial firms. Securities Act of 1933 is passed, requiring registration of new issues and setting disclosure requirements.

1934: Publication of *Security Analysis*, pivotal study on value investing, by Benjamin Graham and Charles Dodd. Securities and Exchange Commission established by Securities Exchange Act of 1934. U.S. Congress imposes limitations on margin loans.

1939: Trust Indenture Act passed. NASD formed as self-regulatory authority for finance industry.

1940: Investment Advisers Act and Investment Company Act passed.

1943: Women work on floor of NYSE due to men being off at war.

1953: New York Curb Exchange renamed American Stock Exchange.

1957: Pacific Stock Exchange formed from merger of Los Angeles and San Francisco exchanges.

1961: Insider trading laws are confirmed in the *Cady, Roberts & Co.* ruling.

1964: William Sharpe devises risk measurement tool, "beta."

1966: Electronic ticker tape displays introduced at NYSE. Securities Investor Protection Corporation created by U.S. Congress to protect against losses from failed brokerage firms.

1967: Muriel Siebert becomes first female NYSE member.

1969: Jerome Pustilnik develops INSTINET, the first electronic trading network to link buyers and sellers anonymously.

1970: Joseph Searles becomes first African American NYSE member.

1971: The NASD launches its automated trading system, called NASDAQ.

1973: Myron Scholes and Fischer Black publish options pricing model theory. Chicago Board of Options Exchange established.

1974: Fidelity Investments offers check writing on investment funds. Commodity Futures Trading Commission established.

1975: Fixed commissions abolished by SEC on "May Day."

1976: Vanguard offers first index fund for individual investors. Alice Jarcho is NYSE's first regular female floor trader. NYSE has its first foreign member, Bruno Des Forges

1977: Merrill Lynch introduces cash management account.

1978: Intermarket Trading System links NYSE and other exchanges. The Amman Financial Market is established in Jordan.

1980: The Stock Exchange of Hong Kong is formed from four smaller exchanges.

1987: Stock market loses 20 percent of its value on October 19.

1988: SEC approves proposals to implement circuit breakers to guard against extreme price movements.

1989: The Bahrain Stock Market is established.

1990: The Shanghai Stock Exchange, which had been closed down by the Communist government, reopens.

1997: Federal Reserve Chairman Alan Greenspan refers to investor's excessively bullish behavior as "irrational exuberance." Japan deregulates commission structures.

1998: NASDAQ merges with AMEX.

1999: Gramm-Leach-Bliley Act removes "Chinese wall" between investment and commercial banking activities for some institutions.

2000: Dow has its biggest one-day gain up to this time, rising 499.19 points on March 16. International Securities Exchange opens for options trading.

2001: The Dow has its biggest one-day loss up to this time, plummeting 684.81 points in the aftermath of terrorist attacks on the World Trade Center.

2002: Sarbanes-Oxley Act becomes law.

2005: Highest price ever is paid for a seat on the NYSE—$4,000,000.

2006: NYSE and Archipelago Holdings, Inc. merge, forming NYSE Group, Inc.

2007: NYSE merges with Euronext, uniting financial markets in Europe and the United States. FINRA created through consolidation of the NYSE regulatory body and NASD. NASDAQ acquires Philadelphia Stock Exchange.

2008: NYSE launches NYSE Realtime Stock Prices, which allows the public to view real-time market data over the Internet. NASDAQ acquires Boston Stock Exchange. The Dow drops 777.68 points on September 29 during the international banking crisis, surpassing the previous record for single day point drop reached on September 17, 2001. The Dow rises by 900 points on October 13, surpassing the previous record for one day point gains of March 16, 2000.

2010: Passage of the The Dodd-Frank Wall Street Reform and Consumer Protection Act, the most sweeping financial reform legislation since the Great Depression.

Chapter 2

State of the Industry

At some point in the past, all roads led to New York City. As the financial center of the world for over a century, Manhattan was the default location for the best investment jobs in America. The top-tier investment firms, banks, and brokerage houses were all domiciled there, clustered around Wall Street in lower Manhattan. Like the sun at the center of a solar system, Wall Street was the source of the coveted jobs from which all great fortunes flowed.

The financial map is a bit more complicated today. New York continues to be a great financial powerhouse, but in an increasingly complex system, it is only one of many hubs. Today's global capital market is more reminiscent of a constellation than a single star. Money capitals have spread out across the globe, from Dubai to Taipei to Mumbai. What this means for candidates is more job options than ever before. Automated trading systems have leveled the playing field, allowing anyone, anywhere, to open a securities firm. Even in the United States the industry can be found just about everywhere. Today, few of the so-called Wall Street firms are actually located on Wall Street. Most people know that Chicago and Boston are important financial centers. Less well known is that Salt Lake City, Seattle, and the Raleigh-Durham Triangle are also hubs, as are Charlotte and Los Angeles, the headquarters of several major brokerage firms. Discount brokerages in particular tend to be headquartered far from Wall Street: Scottrade in St. Louis, Missouri; TD Ameritrade in Omaha, Nebraska; and Charles Schwab in San Francisco, California. Even rural areas and small towns have them. A major investment manager, the Vanguard Group, is tucked into tiny Valley Forge, Pennsylvania. All this makes the term "Wall Street" more a symbol of American stock trading activity than a real location.

With so many options, where does one go to find the best job opportunities? For a start a good rule is the adage, "follow the money." Candidates should keep their eyes on booming economies, new markets, and places where new business formation is strong. Regional investment banks, private equity companies, and venture capital firms are often clustered near the industries they serve. Even in an age when capital crosses state and national borders in the blink of an eye, you can still find local opportunities clustered near centers of economic growth. Community development projects, manufacturing plant construction, and infrastructure improvements typically need bond financing and private lending services. Moreover, as economies grow, so does personal wealth and the need for personal financial advisers to help individuals invest their money.

Let opportunity, not geography, define your job search. Some of the fastest growing economies in the world lie beyond our national border. To find the best and highest paying international finance jobs, take note of global growth trends. The emergence of new capital centers in Asia, Latin America, and Europe abounds with job opportunities, especially in the super-growth nations of China, Brazil, and India. Wherever you find a booming economy, you will also find branches of global investment firms competing alongside local bankers. Of course there are visa, licensing, and regulatory restrictions to working in foreign countries. If these prove insurmountable, consider beginning your career with an American firm and working your way into a job at an international branch.

These are the large trends that will be shaping the careers of young financiers for decades to come. Now what about the foreseeable future? What will happen to the investment job market over the next ten years? And how do prospects look for different types of investment professionals? The Bureau of Labor Statistics (BLS) is a key source for understanding where the market is going. Its *Occupational Outlook Handbook*, 2010–2011 edition, provides a market forecast by occupation for the period 2008 through 2018. The handbook (available in PDF form at no cost to Internet users at http://www.bls.gov) provides insight into the actual state of the American labor market, in contrast to media reports, which could be overstated.

Fast Facts

Foreign Financial Regulatory Authorities

Australia Australian Securities and Investments Commission

Brazil Comissão de Valores Mobiliários

Canada Investment Dealers Association of Canada

France Autorité des Marchés Financiers

Germany Bundesanstalt für Finanzdienstleistungsaufsicht

Italy Commissione Nazionale per le Società e la Borsa

Japan 金融庁

The Netherlands Autoriteit Financiële Markten

The People's Republic of China 中国证券监督管理委员会

Singapore 新加坡金融管理局

Switzerland *French*: Autorité fédérale de surveillance des marchés financiers; *German*: Eidgenössische Finanzmarktaufsicht; *Italian*: Autorità federale di vigilanza sui mercati finanziari.

United Kingdom Financial Services Authority

For example, day-to-day articles about layoffs and unemployment, while true in the short-term, may lead readers to think the long-term industry is weaker than it really is. To get a more accurate picture, it is best to concentrate on the long-term market for a job category.

The handbook forecasts the first three categories—personal financial advisers, financial analysts, and financial examiners—to grow substantially faster than the national average for all occupations through 2018. The fourth category, securities, commodities, and financial services sales agents, will grow at about the same rate as all occupations. The only caveat to keep in mind is that these are broad and general predictions, averaged out among many different job titles. The job with your title may be growing faster or slower than these averages. Therefore, use this data as just one tool among many in your decision-making arsenal.

Overview of Finance Sectors

To operate effectively in the financial field, you need to know the lay of the land—not just your own job duties, but what other divisions, industries and sectors are doing. Because investment pros work so hard at developing their technical skills, they are always at risk of developing tunnel vision, failing to see the big picture—sometimes not even sure what the guy in the next cubicle is doing. This survey of industry types addresses that, explaining the principal activities of each sector.

Investment Banking

An investment bank is a financial institution engaged in several different types of investment activities. It provides advisory services, underwriting services, brokerage services, and research services. Clients are typically large corporations, institutions, governments, and wealthy individuals. Product and service offerings of investment banks vary, depending on size. The largest ones (e.g., Goldman Sachs and J. P. Morgan Chase, both based in New York City) function as "full-service" providers with several lines of business. Called first-tier banks, they have substantial financial resources and engage in the full array of investment banking activities. Their sizeable resources allow them to work with the largest and most powerful governments and corporations in the world. Second-tier investment banks (also known as "middle-market banks") compete by offering fewer lines of business (perhaps three or four), operating in regional markets or having a narrow specialty. Examples include Minneapolis, Minnesota-based Piper Jaffray and Little Rock, Arkansas-based Stephens, Inc. Third-tier firms, often called boutique firms (e.g., Baltimore, Maryland-based Bengur Bryan and Co., and Taglich Brothers, which focuses on microcap companies) serve local needs, offer only one line of business, have a very limited geographic footprint, and/or are narrowly specialized.

Securities Brokerages

Brokerages are firms that handle the massive volume of securities traded on public exchanges. They are the intermediaries between the individual or institutional trader and the exchange. Why do we need brokers? Because the stock exchanges do not allow individuals to walk in and buy a security; they must find a brokerage firm to do that for them. To execute a trade for a client, a broker must be a member of the stock exchange. There are two key types of brokers: traditional stockbrokers and discount brokers. Traditional stockbrokers receive higher commissions in exchange for providing advice and other services to the client investor. Some individuals hire stockbrokers to make all investment decisions for them, based on personal financial goals, while other people ask brokers to merely steer promising investments their way but make the final purchase decision themselves. Either way traditional brokers work with clients on a personal basis, and become familiar with their investing goals and financial wherewithal. Once a decision is made on the investment, the broker sends the order to the floor of the securities exchange by computer. After the transaction is finalized, the broker charges a commission for the service.

Traditional brokers must invest substantial amounts of time finding new clients, as compensation is typically 100 percent commission. Cold-calling, networking, and "dog and pony shows" (financial seminars presented for the purpose of soliciting client business) are typical business development methods. On the other hand a discount broker is a firm that charges a much smaller commission for executing the trade, but provides little to no advice or personal service to the client. Typically the discount firm will have a Web site service that allows investors to do trades via automated trading systems, with no personal interface between the two parties during the transaction. Increasingly, however, the lines between the two types are blurring, with many traditional brokerages offering discounts to high volume clients, and with discount brokers offering ancillary services to their customers.

Venture Capital

Venture capital firms provide capital to start-up or early stage companies with perceived high market potential. In exchange the venture capital firm will receive equity shares in the new venture. Such an investment is highly risky but potentially highly profitable. The venture capital firm will also get significant control over the company's business, essentially becoming the owners of the company, in whole or in part, depending on the percentage of their investment. The new companies are usually formed around a new and innovative product or technology that the venture capitalist believes stands a good chance of market success. The first round of funding is typically called seed funding; the investors who provide these funds are called angels. Later rounds of funding are referred to as second-tier, third-tier, fourth-tier, and so on. Mezzanine funding refers to the capital provided to firms that have become profitable, while bridge funding refers to capital provided to a company for the purpose of taking it public through an IPO. Many venture capital firms invest in a company solely with the intention of taking the company public.

Venture capital firms are expected to provide managerial and technical expertise, as well as funding. In essence, they function as far more than just financiers; they are *incubators* of fledgling firms, providing a wide range of services, including advice on product development, marketing, sales, and systems development. For this reason, venture capital firms usually specialize in a particular market or industry. Some invest only in biotech, high technology, or industrial products; still others fund only new ventures founded by Hispanic or African-American entrepreneurs.

The venture capital industry originated in the United States. It continues to be the largest provider of venture capital to new companies, most of which are domiciled in the United States. However, that trend is diminishing, as American and non-American venture capitalists alike invest in start-ups in other fast-growing countries. The venture capital industries in places like Canada, the United Kingdom, India, and Israel, traditionally insignificant in size, are also growing, fueled by government programs and tax incentives to encourage investments in start-ups.

Investment Management

Investment management is the professional management of various securities (e.g., stocks, bonds) and other assets (e.g., real estate) for the benefit of the client. The investor may be an institution (insurance company, pension fund, corporation) or an individual. The investment management division of an investment bank is generally divided into separate groups, often known as private wealth management and private client services.

A collective investment scheme is a way of investing money with others to participate in a wider range of investments than would be feasible for most individual investors, as well as to share the costs and benefits of doing so. Terminology varies by country; among the terms are mutual funds, investment funds, managed funds, or simply "funds." Collective investment schemes are marketed by focusing on their primary investment objective. For example, some will target a specific geographic region (e.g., emerging markets or Eastern Europe) or an industry sector (e.g., oil and gas or green energy). Investors will pick a fund based on their investment objectives, fees, tax structure and past performance.

Alternative Investments

An alternative investment is an umbrella term that refers to any asset other than "traditional" assets like stocks, bonds, cash, or real estate. Beyond that, there is no universal consensus as to what the term should include. The nontraditional designation can apply to stamps, art, collectibles, luxury goods of all types, antiques, precious metals, even gold (despite gold's history as mankind's most *traditional* form of wealth). But in common parlance, the term usually refers to intangible assets; i.e., hedge funds, managed futures, financial derivatives, commodities, venture capital, and private equity.

Perhaps the most popular alternative investment is the hedge fund. This is a lightly regulated private pool of capital that invests in various types of securities and that pays fees to its manager based on the fund's profitability. For most small investors, hedge funds are high risk and high return. For that reason, they are open only to very wealthy individuals or professional investors (e.g., pension funds or private endowments) who can meet three criteria—(1) have the financial ability to absorb high risk; (2) have large amounts available to invest; and (3) can meet other investment rules stipulated by the fund and/or regulators. Since hedge funds are less subject to regulation (although with the passage of the 2010 Dodd-Frank Act, more of them will be regulated in the future), a loss in value could, at least in theory, wipe out a small investor's entire investment. Risk is elevated by common portfolio practices like short-selling and the widespread use of leverage to supplement investor funds. Other risks include the lack of transparency of financial performance data. Unlike mutual funds, the hedge fund managers themselves may not be subject to regulatory oversight. Nevertheless, for wealthy investors alternative investments can be successfully used for portfolio diversification because their returns are believed to be inversely correlated with traditional stock and bond returns. They further believe that hedge fund risk is reduced by the use of short positions or derivatives to "hedge" the risks inherent in the other investments; this is the concept that gives the asset class its name.

It is difficult to gauge the actual size of the U.S. hedge fund business because data are lacking in the loosely regulated industry.

Everyone
Knows

What Does Blue Chip Mean?

The term blue chip comes from the game of poker. As every card player knows, the blue chips have the highest value, red chips rank second in value, and white chips rank third. Blue chip stocks are those that carry the highest value: the crème de la crème of the stock market. Typically, they are well-established industry leaders with sound financials and high-quality products or services. Their products carry recognizable brand names like Clorox or Kleenex or Coca-Cola. Blue chip stocks are attractive to investors because they have predictable and steady earnings performance with less volatility than many stocks. Although not unaffected by economic downturns, they have the capacity to spring back. For investors who want steady income, blue chips are valued for their ability to pay dividends in any economic climate. Thirty blue chip companies comprise the Dow Jones Industrial Average (DJIA), a leading indicator of stock market performance.

The gambling metaphor does not stop there. Red chip refers to stocks of the People's Republic of China that are incorporated in other countries and listed on the Hong Kong Stock Exchange. The Hang Seng China-Affiliated Corporations Index is an index of 30 red chip stocks; i.e., the Chinese equivalent of the DJIA. A purple chip stock is a Chinese hybrid of red and blue chips that is listed on the Hong Kong Stock Exchange. Green chip is a term widely bandied about since 2004, and as you might expect, refers to the so-called "green" environmentally friendly companies.

However one thing is crystal clear: *hedge funds are hot*, both as an investment and as a career opportunity. In the last two decades hedge fund activity has hit an all-time high, fueled by the enormous returns they have been known to generate. Compensation structures can be very high, even for managers in their twenties or thirties, and the possibility of earning millions per year is not a complete fantasy. Although many hedge fund professionals earn considerably less, the promise of generous compensation will continue to attract eager recruits for years to come.

Employment Outlook: 2008 to 2018

Periodic (e.g., month-to-month) employment in the securities industry is tied to two key factors. The first and most important one is the state of the economy. Hiring will usually be up during bull markets and economic booms and down during bear markets and recessions. Nevertheless as noted above, candidates should not be overly discouraged (or overly optimistic) about the immediate state of the economy or stock market. Monthly hiring trends provide a snapshot of the short term, but are not a good guide for those planning a multi-decade career. Second, regulatory reform can affect hiring trends, although the impact can be either positive or negative. On the one hand, regulation can effectively put some companies out of business if they are not able to pay for the costs of compliance or if their business practices have been upended by a new rule. More likely, however, is that regulation will lead to more employment demand. As securities firms gear up to comply with the new regulations, they will usually need to hire more skilled labor to assist in updating their internal systems and processes.

Job Outlook by Occupation

Below find capsule descriptions of various jobs predicted to increase in availability over the next 10 years.

Personal Financial Advisers (BLS 13-2052)
This category covers jobs that dispense advice on securities-related matters, such as portfolio mix, financial planning, tax and investment strategies, and the like. Included are people who work in this capacity at investment banks, brokerages, private banks, wealth management firms, and venture capital firms. The task of a financial

adviser is to develop a personal financial plan by examining a client's individual net worth, assets, liabilities, cash flow, tax status, and financial goals. In 2008 personal financial advisers held 208,400 jobs in all parts of the United States, though a substantial number of them were located in the states of New York, California, and Florida. About 63 percent worked in the finance and insurance industries, including securities and commodity brokerages, banks, insurance carriers, and financial investment firms. About 29 percent of the group was self-employed, operating small investment advisory firms or working as independent consultants.

Personal financial advisers are a fast-growing category, with jobs expected to grow much faster than the average for all U.S. occupations. Between 2008 and 2018, jobs will grow by 30 percent to a total of 271,200, an increase of 62,800 jobs. This phenomenon can be explained by several factors. In the first place, the baby boom generation will soon be reaching retirement. More and more advisers will be needed to service the huge numbers of boomers in need of retirement planning services. Second, many companies have replaced traditional pension plans with retirement savings programs, effectively shifting the burden of retirement onto the employee. Yet a significant number of employees do not have the expertise to manage their own retirement plans. This will drive the job market for advisers to manage employees' portfolios. Third, longer life spans will increase demand, as consumers are forced to manage their investments longer and more aggressively to meet their financial needs in old age. A fourth key trend is the rising complexity of investment products and services. Experts will be needed to understand and manage products that are increasingly beyond the educational level of many laymen. Finally the rising number of high net worth individuals is a promising trend. Both the sheer volume of very wealthy individuals and the higher asset levels of each of them will drive demand for private advisers and wealth managers.

Even with strong job growth, however, the financial adviser field is highly competitive. High pay scales and generous compensation will continue to make this occupation a magnet for new entrants. A common career path is to enter the field by working for a bank or full-service brokerage. Having a background in sales is helpful, since people with strong selling skills are usually the most successful financial advisers. A college degree and certification can lend further credibility. Yet compared to other financial professions like investment banking, the barriers to entry are relatively low. Those with proper certification can enter the field simply by working as independents or at small advisory firms. This ease of entry combined with high compensation will continue to attract many new candidates in years to come.

Financial Analysts (BLS 13-2051)

Financial analysts provide a valuable service to individual and institutional investors. They analyze the performance of stocks, bonds, commodities, and other types of assets for the purpose of determining if the investment is promising. In 2008 financial analysts held 250,600 jobs in the United States, of which approximately 47 percent worked in the finance and insurance industries, including securities and commodity brokers, banks and credit institutions, and insurance carriers.

Employment of financial analysts is also expected to grow much faster than the average for all U.S. occupations. Although not as robust as the growth rate for financial advisers, analyst jobs will increase by 20 percent during the 2008–18 decade, adding 49,600 jobs for a total of 300,300. Several factors explain the growth, the most important of which is simply the overall higher expected level of assets under management: i.e., the more investments there are, the more analysts will be needed. Other factors include the growing complexity of investment products, which will require expert analysis to understand. Also, as new types of mutual and hedge funds are introduced over the next decade, more financial analysts will be needed to research and identify promising investments. Globalism will add another dimension of complexity to the investment process, as unfamiliar foreign markets, financial products, and regulatory environments expand the need for expertise. Nevertheless, even with expanding opportunities there will be significant competition for these high-paying jobs, especially for junior analysts. The best way to compete is to present the strongest academic background possible, with rigorous training in economics, finance, and accounting. Candidates with special expertise in international issues will be better positioned than most. An applicant's prospects will be further improved if he or she can present certified financial analyst certification and a master's degree in economics, finance, or business.

Financial Examiners (BLS 13-2061)

The financial examiner category includes those whose job is to ensure compliance with laws and regulations governing securities institutions and exchanges. The majority of them work for the Federal executive branch, state governments, the central monetary authorities (SEC, Federal Reserve Bank, Office of the Comptroller of the Currency), and as intermediaries for depositary institutions and securities and commodities brokers. Most of the 26,050 jobs in this category are found in the District of Columbia, Nebraska, Massachusetts, Delaware, and Minnesota.

The BLS does not provide a percentage growth figure for the financial examiner category; it simply projects that 2008-2018 employment will grow "much faster than the average" for all U.S. occupations. Based on the other two forecasts, we can extrapolate that the same factors underlying growth in them will also fuel growth in financial examiners, who will be needed to track industry activities. The District of Columbia tops the list in terms of annual mean wages at $126,410, followed by Illinois at $91,170 and New York at $88,780. While one might assume that the District of Columbia would be the site of most of these public sector jobs, Massachusetts holds the lead, followed by Minnesota and Nebraska.

Securities, Commodities, and Financial Services Sales Agents (BLS 41-3031)

This category covers any job title involved in the buying and selling of securities, or those which receive compensation for providing services, such as securities advice and counseling. This group held about 317,200 jobs in 2008, with about 49 percent of jobs in the securities, commodity contracts, and other investment industries. About 15 percent of these workers were self-employed. Unlike the three categories discussed above, securities sales agents are projected to grow at average, rather than superior, rates over the ten-year period. From 2008 to 2018, employment is projected to grow about 9 percent, which is about as fast as the average for all U.S. occupations. By 2018, the total number of jobs will be 346,700, an increase of 29,600 jobs. The key factor restraining growth will be continued consolidation of the industry resulting from the impact of global economic problems since the fall of 2008 on the financial services industry. Not only will firms eliminate duplicative jobs, streamline operations, and reduce hiring, they are expected to lay off workers to trim budgets. Additionally industry deregulation may change the pattern and volume of job growth. For example, as traditional barriers between depositary and investment banks crumble, the result may be more market players and increased competition, resulting in a smaller market share for each. Deregulation may also lead to more acquisitions of brokerages and investment houses by depositary banks, also resulting in consolidated operations and lower demand for workers. Even the Internet seems likely to play a role in reducing job demand in this category. Online investment and portfolio management is resulting in reduced need for brokers to manage clients' day-to-day needs.

This employment category will be subject to intense competition, as applicants vie for a reduced number of job openings. The continued promise of high incomes and compensation packages will continue to make these jobs very popular. The consequence of fewer openings is that applicants must present better credentials and skills than ever before. An applicant who can present one or more certifications, licenses, and graduate degrees, such as an MBA in finance or business, will stand a better chance of getting hired. Having a degree from an Ivy League or high ranked business school will also improve a candidate's prospects, as can outstanding grades in finance, economics, and business courses.

For those with less attractive credentials or educational records, the best bet is to consider small or regional firms. While industry consolidation has reduced the number of openings at the large securities firms, the second and third-tier firms are less affected by this trend. This career strategy is especially smart for those interested in sales jobs with the intensely competitive investment banking industry, which, even in normal times, has high barriers to entry.

Federal Regulatory Framework

The purpose of regulation is to maintain the integrity of the financial system. This umbrella goal means many things: enforcing securities laws, investigating complaints against industry professionals, prosecuting individuals or companies that break industry rules, licensing providers of financial services, and protecting the investing public. In a nutshell, federal regulators seek to maintain public confidence in the nation's financial markets so that they operate smoothly and fairly.

The American financial regulatory system has taken about two centuries to reach its current form. It is a response to the systemic turmoil and instability that occurred in past epochs of the nation's financial history. The country has collectively learned through trial and error that financial markets left unregulated are subject to exploitation and domination by the privileged few. Today's regulatory framework aims to level the playing field. That lofty goal does not always work in practice; nevertheless, it is something to which the nation aspires. How does financial regulation affect people who work day-to-day in the industry? It affects everything they do. Any person or company that buys, sells, or deals in securities for public consumption must be licensed by a national or state regulatory authority and is subject to its rules and regulations. With only a few exceptions, all financial products sold in the United States are regulated by federal and state government authorities.

Securities and Exchange Commission

The Securities and Exchange Commission (SEC) is the chief regulatory body for the securities industry. It has the power to license and regulate stock exchanges, the companies whose securities are traded on them, and the brokers and dealers who conduct the trading. To ensure that investors have accurate information about the stocks they buy, the SEC enforces laws governing corporate reporting and disclosure. It is also mandated to prevent corporate abuses relating to the offering and sale of securities. The following are the seven federal statutes that serve as the backbone of the SEC's regulation of the investment and securities industry.

Securities Act of 1933

Prior to the 1929 stock market crash, securities trading was regulated by state blue-sky laws. In its aftermath, the *Securities Act of 1933* was passed, which shifted regulation to federal authorities. Often referred to as the "truth in securities" law, the act has two core objectives: to make sure that investors receive financial and other relevant information about securities traded in public markets, and to prohibit the sale of securities by any form of misrepresentation, misinformation, or fraud. This means that a company must disclose any information needed by investors to make informed investment decisions.

A primary means of accomplishing these goals is through the registration of securities. Companies are required to fill out forms that ask them to disclose certain key facts, such as descriptions of the company's business, its management, and officers, as well as describing the security to be offered for sale. The company's financial statements must be certified by independent auditors and attached to the registration form. A *prospectus*—the document to which an issuer's securities are marketed to a potential investor—is generally filed in conjunction with the registration statement.

The SEC is the enforcement arm for insuring compliance with the law and has the right to examine registration statements for adherence with disclosure requirements. It is illegal for a company to submit false information or to omit material facts about its offering. Doing so could lead to civil liability and monetary penalties for the violator. However, the SEC does not guarantee that the information is accurate. Any investor who buys the security and sustains a

On the Cutting
Edge

Passing Fads: Celebrity Stock Indices

No, the Angelina Jolie Stock Index is not the invention of *People* magazine or Entertainment Tonight. It is a serious benchmark tooled by a serious market watcher, just like the Lindsay Lohan Stock Index, the Eva Longoria Stock Index and the Paris Hilton Stock Index. The Jolie Index was dreamed up by Stockerblog (http://stockerblog.blogspot.com), and has included major NYSE companies (like Disney [DIS], Sony [SNE], Viacom [VIA-B] and Time Warner [TWX]) that have some connection with Jolie's films. The theory is that you can bank on the high earning power of her films and any company affiliated with her. In the case of the Lohan Index, stocks may be picked solely by virtue of the namesake's implied or actual endorsement. For example, if Lohan drives a Mercedes-Benz, the theory is that fans will buy one also, thereby increasing sales and winning Daimler AG (FWB:DAI) a place in her index.

Unfortunately, the theory does not seem to work very well in the real world. Even when linked to one of the brightest stars in Hollywood, the Jolie Index has at times lagged the DJIA. The Lohan Index declined after its star went into drug rehab. There is also the transient nature of fame and the fickleness of the celebrity-obsessed public, which can take the bloom off stocks really fast (and do not discount the potential market impact of celebrity crime: two of the above stars have served jail time).

So exercise caution when placing your trust in celebrity stock indices. Their value as measurement tools can shift as rapidly as the latest fads.

loss has the right to seek recovery under the 1933 Act—if, of course, he or she can prove that the loss resulted from the erroneous or misleading reporting.

Not all offerings of securities must be registered with the SEC. Private offerings (i.e., securities not offered to the general public but sold "privately" to a limited number of individual or institutional investors) are exempt. Intrastate offerings (sale of securities made solely to residents of a single state by a company both a resident and doing business in that state) are exempt from registration. Sales of securities issued by municipal, state, and federal governments are exempt. There are also provisions in the law for exemption of certain small businesses. Offerings up to $5 million are exempt subject to SEC approval and review.

Securities Exchange Act of 1934

The Securities Exchange Act of 1934 was the legislation that created the Securities and Exchange Commission. It defines the powers the SEC has over the securities industry. This includes the power to register, regulate, and oversee brokerage firms, transfer agents, and clearing agencies. The SEC also has jurisdiction over the nation's financial self-regulatory organizations (SROs), which includes the Financial Industry Regulatory Authority (formerly NASDAQ), and all the stock exchanges, including the New York Stock Exchange and the American Stock Exchange. The act also identifies and prohibits certain types of conduct in the markets and provides the commission with disciplinary powers over regulated entities and persons associated with them.

Additionally the 1934 act spells out the laws that govern four key industry issues: corporate reporting, proxy solicitations, tender offers, insider trading, and the registration of SROs, associations, and other industry groups. Regarding corporate reporting, the act empowers the SEC to require periodic reporting of information by companies that have publicly traded securities. Companies with more than $10 million in assets whose securities are held by more than 500 owners must file annual and other periodic reports. Most companies are now required to file electronically on an electronic registration system, Electronic Data Gathering, Analysis, and Retrieval, commonly known as the "EDGAR" database. The company will first file registration statements and a prospectus on EDGAR at the time they register with the SEC. Periodic financial information is provided via the filing of a Form 10-K or 10-KSB, which contains much of the same information you would find in an annual report. This makes access by investors and the general public easy and efficient and cuts down on the paper glut. Only those companies claiming a hardship exemption are permitted to bypass EDGAR and file on paper. In 2002, EDGAR filing requirements was expanded to include filings of foreign companies and governments. EDGAR can be accessed through the SEC Web site at http://www.sec.gov.

The Securities Exchange Act also governs proxy solicitations, materials used to solicit shareholders' votes in annual or special meetings held for the election of directors and the approval of other corporate action. This information, contained in proxy materials, must be filed with the Commission in advance of any solicitation to ensure compliance with the disclosure rules. Solicitations, whether by management or shareholder groups, must disclose all important facts concerning the issues on which holders are asked to vote. The act also requires disclosure of important information by anyone seeking to acquire more than 5 percent of a company's securities by direct purchase or tender offer. Such an offer often is extended in an effort to gain control of the company. As with rules governing proxy solicitations, this allows shareholders to make informed decisions on critical corporate events.

The act further deals with the issue of fraud in securities lending. It broadly prohibits fraudulent activities of any kind in connection with the offer, purchase, or sale of securities. These provisions are the basis for many types of disciplinary actions. One of the best known of them is insider trading, which is an illegal act wherein a person trades a security while in possession of material nonpublic information, and where that person has a duty to withhold the information or refrain from trading. An example of this is the officer of the company whose stock is being traded. All officers are in possession of nonpublic information and thus are legally prohibited from trading in the security based on information of which the general public has no knowledge. Last, the act regulates all types of SROs. They are also required to file disclosure statements that must be periodically updated. Although industry rules and procedures are developed by the SRO, they must be cleared by the SEC in advance.

Trust Indenture Act of 1939

The Trust Indenture Act is a law passed in 1939 that aims to protect the rights of bond investors. It applies to debt securities like bonds, debentures, and notes offered for public sale, and is applicable to issues more than $5 million in value. The act stipulates that an indenture or formal written agreement is required between the bond issuer and bondholder that fully discloses the details of the issue. Even though the securities may be registered, they may not be offered for sale to the public unless there is an indenture between the issuer and investor. It also requires that a trustee be appointed for each bond issue. The trustee acts on behalf of investors, protects their interests, and may seize the bond issuer's assets in the event of bankruptcy or insolvency.

Investment Company Act of 1940

The Investment Company Act of 1940 regulates the organization of companies that are engaged in the investment and trading of securities and which sell securities to the general public. It is the prime law regulating mutual fund companies, although the term "investment company" includes other types of firms as well. At the time the act was passed by Congress, mutual funds were still very new. The act defined a mutual fund and established standards for what it could and could not do. The objective of the 1940 act is to minimize conflicts of interest that may occur within an investment company. To guard against this, the act requires investment firms to disclose their financial status and investment practices to all investors any time a security is sold and periodically as well. This includes disclosing material information about the fund, its past performance, and investment objectives.

In addition to regulating mutual funds, the act defines and regulates face-amount certificate companies (investment companies that issue face-amount certificates) and unit investment trusts (investment companies organized as a trust indenture or other contract of custodianship, and which issues redeemable securities only). The act generally applies to all investment companies, but does exempt some types. Its best known exemption is a hedge fund. However, parts of the 1940 act have been revised by the Dodd-Frank Wall Street Reform and Consumer Protection Act of 2010. As discussed below the 2010 law will for the first time put many hedge funds and private equity firms under a regulatory framework.

Investment Advisers Act of 1940

The Investment Advisers Act of 1940 is the most important law for those beginning a career in investment. It deals with what you need to know about the requirements for registration. The act generally stipulates that firms or individuals who are compensated for giving advice about securities investments must register with the SEC. This includes people who make recommendations, write investment reports, publish investment reports, or otherwise furnish analyses of securities, whether those analyses are oral or written. There are numerous exceptions to this rule. Only advisers who manage $25 million or more, or who advise a registered investment company, need register. Advisers managing less than this amount must generally register with state securities authorities. Although state-registered advisers are governed primarily by state law, several provisions of the federal Investment Advisers Act of 1940 apply to them.

Since there are other exemptions and prohibitions to the rule and since the law is subject to interpretation, interested parties would be advised to seek legal counsel if they are unsure as to whether they need to register. An employee of an SEC-registered investment adviser does not need to register separately in most cases. Surprisingly, you do not need to be engaged full-time in the investment business to be required to register. One need only hold himself out to the public as an investment adviser. Then there are the gray area professions, like college finance professors, accountants, lawyers, publishers of financial newsletters, publishers of mass-circulation financial newspapers, and the like. Although these would generally not be required to register, it is always wise to have your case reviewed by qualified counsel.

A key exclusion to the registration rule is broker-dealers. If providing advice is incidental to one's job description or business and you do not receive special compensation for advice per se, then you, as a broker-dealer, do not need to register. Another exemption has to do with the location of one's client base. If all of your clients are in the same state as your principal place of business, then you would qualify for an exemption. Other exemptions include advisers who do not issue advice about securities listed on a national exchange, whose only clients are insurance companies, who have had less than 15 clients in the past 12 months, and who give advice solely to charitable nonprofit organizations. Last, registration with the SEC as an investment adviser is not just a requirement, but also a right. That privilege may be revoked for engaging in securities fraud.

Securities Investor Protection Act of 1970

INTERVIEW

Socially Responsible Investing

Steve Lydenberg
Partner, Strategic Vision, Domini Social Investments

What is socially responsible investing (also known as "green investing")?

Socially responsible investing (SRI) is about using finance to create a fairer and more sustainable world. By making sustainability part of their investment decisions, responsible investors encourage corporations to act more accountably, and to help the environment and society, not hurt it. The three basic aspects of socially responsible investing are these:

- Applying social, environmental, and governance standards to investment portfolios
- Engaging in direct dialogue with corporations
- Investing in community development initiatives

Social investors use all three. While each has a different purpose and impact, each strengthens the impact of the others.

Investing is a purchasing decision. Caring about it is like caring about what you eat or how you choose to lead your life. If you are a high school teacher, it might well strike you as inconsistent to invest in alcohol manufacturers that advertise to youth. If you support environmental causes, then it is only being consistent to invest in companies that are not causing environmental harm. Consistency is one of the most common reasons people start down the path to responsible investing.

Along with applying standards to their investment portfolios, social investors engage with companies on social and environmental issues through letter-writing, direct dialogue, proxy voting, and the filing of shareholder resolutions. Shareholder activism makes corporate managers aware that their investors want real change and thoughtful long-term management, as well as profits. Today, corporations do not generally hear about social and environmental issues from their other shareholders, who are only interested in making money. Social investors have helped to change that.

In addition, social investors place deposits with community development financial institutions (CDFIs), including community development banks and credit unions. In this way, they can channel their money directly to projects that serve neighborhoods and regions of great need by creating, among other things, low-income housing, loans to small entrepreneurs, financial literacy, and by providing affordable financial services for those who lack access to the mainstream banking system.

What criteria do you use to identify companies that are socially responsible?

Responsible investors generally seek to invest in companies that have strong relations with their stakeholders, including companies that invest in their employees, set high standards for their suppliers, serve the greatest needs of their local communities, manage their environmental affairs responsibly, and monitor the human rights implications of their activities.

Many socially responsible investors also favor companies involved in clean technology and energy efficiency, alternative energy, microfinance, mobile communications, organic agriculture, vaccines, and healthcare products. Many socially responsible investors avoid companies substantially involved in:

- Nuclear weapons, landmines, and cluster bombs
- Tobacco, gambling, and alcohol
- Firearms
- Nuclear power

Responsible investors may also avoid companies that have patterns of environmental harm, substantial worker safety violations, involvement in human rights abuses, major consumer product controversies, or suppliers who consistently abuse their workers.

There is a popular conception that socially responsible investments are not as profitable as other investments. How do you respond to this?

Socially responsible investment firms have many different approaches, and the returns they produce vary depending on these approaches and the skills of the portfolio managements. However, the majority of studies have shown that a socially responsible investment approach need not detract from investment performance. Of course, all investment strategies are subject to risk, including loss of principal. SRI is no different. Many of us believe that social and environmental standards help identify companies with high quality management, positive corporate cultures, and socially and environmentally beneficial products—in short, companies that are built to last.

What are the pros and cons of working in the socially responsible finance industry?

Companies that specialize in socially responsible investing tend to be smaller than the mainstream financial companies. For someone who prefers a smaller company with a collegial working atmosphere, SRI may be a good fit. And because SRI companies are interested in a variety of social and environmental issues, they may be more

(continued on next page)

INTERVIEW

Socially Responsible Investing
(continued)

intellectually stimulating for someone whose interests extend beyond the bottom line.

In a similar way, the entire SRI field in the U.S. is relatively small, and so it is fairly easy to get to know the major players—for instance, by attending SRI in the Rockies or the Social Investment Forum's annual conference, both major industry conferences.

It is probably safe to say that socially responsible investment firms tend not to offer the outsized compensation packages that you see at some of the mainstream financial firms. But many feel that the opportunity to contribute to a better world makes a career in SRI worthwhile.

The socially responsible investment sector has been around now for about 30 years. How has it changed in that time period?
The earliest socially responsible investors were religious people who were motivated by a wish not to invest in businesses that they saw as destructive to society. Therefore the emphasis was on avoiding industries such as alcohol, tobacco, and gambling, or companies involved in military contracting. Later investors were also motivated by political, humanitarian, and sustainability convictions, which led them, for instance, to seek divestment from companies doing business with the apartheid regime in South Africa, and which has made environmental considerations one of the mainstays of the social investment process.

As time goes by, more and more data has become available on the environmental, social, and governance performance of companies,

The Securities Investor Protection Act of 1970 established the Securities Investor Protection Corporation (SIPC). This is another non-profit private sector SRO with a federal government mandate. The SIPC does not regulate the conduct of the securities industry but serves a vital role in the aftermath of a brokerage firm's failure or bankruptcy. It helps customers of the failed firm recoup their losses, whether caused by fraud, misappropriation, mismanagement, or other reasons. However investors are only protected if a broker-dealer sometimes abbreviated as ESG. Today's socially responsible investors are interested not just in avoiding companies that are destructive to people and the planet. They want to invest in companies that have a positive impact.

In recent years, social investment firms have developed more sophisticated ways to assess the performance of the companies they invest in. Some have also developed new vehicles for SRI investing, such as environmental and clean energy sector funds, or innovative approaches to traditional vehicles—like the Domini Social Bond Fund, which invests up to 10 percent of its portfolio in CDFIs.

What type of educational background would you recommend for a person who wants to work in the socially responsible arena of investment?
For those who are interested in being researchers or analysts, some educational background in business, finance, or economics is helpful, but we also welcome candidates with undergraduate degrees or experience in environmental science, other sciences, or the humanities.

For those who are interested in portfolio management, a strong background in finance and accounting is important, and the Chartered Financial Analyst certification is a strong credential.

What type of life and work experience do you like to see in candidates who apply to your firm?
When evaluating potential researchers and analysts, we look for solid writing and research skills, familiarity with social and environmental issues, and strong organizational skills. Foreign languages are helpful—especially Japanese, since Japanese companies make up a large proportion of the Asian stock markets. Many people come to SRI after working for nonprofit environmental or human rights organizations, a background that is most helpful in understanding the often complicated issues relating to corporations' social and environmental policies and practices.

fails. They are not protected against losses suffered from investing in securities.

The SIPC will typically ask a federal court to appoint a trustee to liquidate the firm and protect its customers, who will receive the distributions of cash and securities. The SIPC also provides insurance coverage to investors up to $500,000 of the net balance. However, not all types of securities are protected by the SIPC. Cash and securities generally are covered, but such things as commodity futures, currency, fixed annuity, and unregistered contracts are not. Most brokers and dealers registered under the Securities Exchange Act of 1934 are required to be members of the SIPC. Understanding the function of the SIPC is vital for anyone engaged in the trading of public securities, and it may also be a source of employment ideas.

Public Company Accounting Reform and Corporate Responsibility Act of 2002 (Sarbanes-Oxley Act)

Most, if not all, federal financial regulatory laws are passed in response to a financial scandal or abuse of some sort. The Sarbanes-Oxley Act of 2002 ("Sox") is no exception. Following accounting scandals at Enron, Tyco International, and WorldCom Corporations in the late 1990s and early 2000s, Sox was enacted to address the problems that had led to the abuses; namely, by increasing financial disclosure rules and enhancing standards for corporate accountability. In this case and unlike other SEC laws, the investor or investment professional (fund manager, broker-dealer, adviser) is generally not the target of regulation. Instead, they are the beneficiaries of it. By strengthening corporate accounting controls, Sox improves the quality of company information provided to investors. It also lays down criminal and civil penalties for corporations that violate its provisions, and additional penalties for retaliation against whistleblowers who attempt to expose accounting irregularities.

Although the law essentially deals with internal corporate issues, its passage has had a marked impact on the securities markets. The scandals caused the collapse of some of the country's largest and most prominent corporations, causing precipitous drops in share prices and staggering losses on the stock market. The passage of Sox helped restore public confidence in the nation's stock markets. Investors have also benefitted from improved accuracy and transparency of financial reporting. The more confident investors are in the reliability and truthfulness of the financial statement, the better their investment positions will be.

The 2002 passage of Sarbanes-Oxley was followed by similar legislation in other countries. In Australia the Corporate Law Economic Reform Program Act or CLERP-9 was passed in 2004. In Japan, the Financial Instruments and Exchange Law was passed in 2006 and is popularly known as J-Sox (though it also deals with other key industry issues, like registration of broker dealers). The Financial Security Law of France was passed in 2003. Passed by the Canadian legislature in 2003 was another comprehensive piece of securities legislation, Bill 198, which dealt with corporate governance and disclosure, hence giving it the nickname of C-Sox. These developments demonstrate how interconnected the global capital markets truly are, and how events in one country's market can reverberate across the world.

Rules and Regulations

In addition to the seven statutes above, the industry is governed by numerous SEC amendments, revisions, releases, staff interpretations, and updates that have been passed since the original laws went into effect. These are listed on the SEC's Web site under *Rules and Regulations for the Securities and Exchange Commission and Major Securities Laws.* The site also summarizes key areas of the statutes that pertain to members' professional conduct and practices.

Dodd-Frank Wall Street Reform and Consumer Protection Act of 2010 (Dodd-Frank Act)

The 2010 Dodd-Frank Act was brought about by the so-called "Great Recession" of the late 2000s. A sweeping piece of legislation affecting many areas of the banking and investment industries, the act modifies many rules of conduct for investment firms and individuals. Although too complex to review in detail here, the law has two key changes. Prior to 2010 investment advisers with fewer than 15 clients during the previous 12 months and that did not present themselves to the public as investment advisers were not required to register with the SEC. Under terms of the new law that exemption is cancelled. This subjects many additional investment advisers, hedge funds, and private equity firms to registration requirements, including many entities that had never been required to register before. Also, a sub-section of the Act, known as the Private Fund Investment Advisers Registration Act, establishes rules and regulations for private funds, hedge funds, and similar investment vehicles. This effectively closes reporting loopholes that the historically unregulated hedge fund industry had used to limit or avoid certain types of information disclosure.

National Futures Association (formerly, the Commodity Futures Trading Commission)

Congress created the Commodity Futures Trading Commission (CFTC) in 1974 as an independent agency with the authority to regulate commodity futures and options markets in the United States. Since then, the organization has undergone many changes, including a name change. The reason for the title change is fairly obvious: the word "commodity" had become outdated. At the time the CFTC was created in 1974, most futures trading involved agricultural products. Over the years the concept expanded to include a vast number of other products, including purely financial "intangible" products. This meant that the organization was regulating products from the proverbial "pork bellies" to the most complex financial contract imaginable. That led Congress to authorize the futures industry to create an SRO to redefine itself and expand its regulatory mission. The result was the founding in 1982 of the National Futures Association (NFA), which aimed to do for futures what FINRA had done for stocks: i.e., serve as a self-regulatory body responsible for protecting the public and investors from fraud, market manipulation, and other abusive trading practices related to futures and options. The law was updated again in 2000 by the Commodity Futures Modernization Act. Today, the NFA is the chief watchdog of the industry and is the first stop on the career path of all futures professionals. It is the primary forum for resolving investor complaints through mediation and arbitration. As a nod to its agricultural past, the modern NFA is still headquartered in Chicago, the city that was once the site of farmers' trading markets, and which is today the headquarters of CME Group (i.e., the entity that now includes the Chicago Board of Trade and Chicago Mercantile Exchange).

Any person or organization that intends to work as a futures professional must register with the NFA pursuant to the Commodity Exchange Act. If your plan is to be a principal, floor broker, floor trader, introducing broker, futures commission merchant, commodity pool operator, commodity trading adviser, associated person, or agricultural trade-option merchant, then you will probably need to register. Depending on title, registration may require submission of an application form, a fingerprint card, the payment of a fee and dues, the submission of a financial statement certified by an independent public accountant, and a proficiency exam. The standard proficiency exam is the Series 3 (National Commodity Futures Examination) administered by FINRA (see next section). If you want to become a branch manager, introducing broker or take on other added responsibilities, you must take the Series 30 (Branch Manager Exam), Series 31 (Futures Managed Funds Exam) or Series 32 (Limited Futures Exam). There are, of course, a number of exceptions

Best Practice

What Does a Private Equity Analyst Do?

Mainly a lot of research and analytics while sitting in a cubicle. Private equity analysts "crunch the numbers" on potential deals; i.e., do a spreadsheet analysis of the cost and benefits of investing in the company. They may also carry out due diligence on the target's management, prepare background materials for partners, find new deals through industry research, and prepare a final report that reaches a conclusion on the prospect based on their analysis of all the findings. All in all, the work is tedious and detailed, requiring long hours and intensive labor. A lot of work will require the analyst to be chained to the desk. Nevertheless the job has a glamorous side too: analysts, even entry level ones, are in continual contact with the target's executives, lawyers, and consultants. Networking and schmoozing events come with the territory. Astute analysts will take advantage of the opportunity to deepen their relationships with the partners and show them what they can do. All in all, analysts can emerge from the experience with a solid foundation in how businesses work, fully prepared for the next stage of their private equity career.

to the registration requirement. You can get additional information on exemptions by referring to the Commodity Exchange Act or by contacting the NFA registration staff.

Financial Industry Regulatory Authority

FINRA is the security industry's largest SRO. It is a relatively recent entrant to the regulatory framework, created in 2007 from a series of mergers and acquisitions. Its primary predecessor body was the NASD. FINRA was formed by a consolidation of the NASD with NYSE Regulation, Inc., the latter of which was the enforcement, arbitration, and regulatory unit of the New York Stock Exchange. Like other SROs, FINRA is a private sector organization, but with its authority and duties derived from the SEC. Its general purpose is to ensure that the financial markets operate fairly and smoothly, and to provide regulatory oversight of its member firms and exchange markets. FINRA's jurisdiction covers all types of publicly traded securities, including equities, corporate bonds, futures, and options. Although its membership numbers are constantly changing, as of 2011 it had regulatory powers over approximately 5,100 brokerage firms and 676,000 registered securities representatives. As a regulator of exchange markets, it oversees the NYSE (including NYSE Arca, the electronic trading platform for options and stocks), the International Securities Exchange, over-the-counter markets, and NASDAQ, the latter of which includes all NASDAQ's previous acquisitions—the American Stock Exchange, the Boston Stock Exchange, and the Philadelphia Stock Exchange.

Today, FINRA executes a broad array of functions for the securities industry. Its core responsibilities are to license individuals and to admit firms to the industry. FINRA is tasked with writing the membership requirements for gaining admission to the industry and the rules, regulations, and standards of conduct for its members. All firms dealing in securities sold to the public that are not regulated by another SRO (e.g., the Municipal Securities Rulemaking Board) are required to be members. FINRA also may periodically examine its members' operations to ensure regulatory compliance. As the organization that administers the Series 7 and other licensing exams, it is typically the first regulatory body encountered by new entrants to the profession. FINRA is also a provider of educational services, both to the public and its members. Professional training and test preparation are two of its key educational service offerings. Other FINRA functions include providing arbitration and dispute resolution services and selling regulatory products and services to stock exchanges.

Pursuant to its SEC mandate, FINRA is delegated the authority to discipline registered representatives and member firms that fail to comply with its rules and regulations. It can levy substantial fines against member firms that are found in violation of its rules. In 2009, the most recent year for which data is available, it levied nearly $50 million in fines and ordered $8.2 million in restitution to be paid to investors. FINRA is also mandated to arbitrate disputes between its members and client investors. Nevertheless, its disciplinary authority is much more limited than that of the SEC. In the aftermath of the near-collapse of the financial system in 2008, FINRA was criticized for its perceived lax enforcement and seeming failure to detect the abuses that led to the near-collapse.

FINRA is such a new organization that as of 2011, it had yet to complete a consolidated rulebook for its members. It is in the process of merging and rewriting the rules of its incorporated entities, including the former NASD and NYSE Regulation. Until that redrafted rulebook is complete and has been approved, members will be subject to a "Transitional Rulebook," a temporary document that combines rules of both former entities. However, the incorporated NYSE Rules in the Transitional Rulebook apply only to FINRA members that are also members of NYSE, while the former NASD Rules generally apply to all FINRA members. All FINRA members are subject to the FINRA By-Laws and Schedules to the By-Laws. Below is a brief description of three of the most common FINRA proficiency exams.

Series 7: Commonly known as the general securities representative license, the Series 7 authorizes licensees to sell just about any type of individual security. This includes common stocks, preferred stocks, put and call options, bonds, and other fixed income instruments, and many more. The exceptions to the rule are real estate, life insurance and commodities futures, which Series 7 licensees may not sell. To obtain this license, applicants must pass the Series 7 exam, a six-hour comprehensive test covering a wide variety of topics in investment, securities, trading, rules of conduct, professional ethics, and government regulations. A technical understanding of complex investment finance is essential, as the exam will cover advanced topics in options and equities. People who pass the test become a FINRA registered representative. However, you do not need to be employed as a stockbroker to be a Series 7 licensee; financial planners and other advisers may also hold the license.

Series 6: This license allows its holders to sell packaged investment products such as mutual funds, variable annuities, and unit investment trusts. The Series 6 exam is much shorter and less comprehensive than the Series 7: only 135 minutes long versus six hours for the Series 7 exam. Test topics include technical questions about packaged products, as well as about the ethics, standards and regulations pertaining to them. The Series 7 exam is required for insurance agents if securities constitute the underlying investments within the products they sell.

Series 3: This license authorizes holders to sell commodity futures contracts. Series 3 licensees tend to specialize in commodities and sell no other products. The Series 3 exam is also a very short test— about two hours long—but not necessarily easy, as it covers technical topics on one of the riskiest and complex financial instruments sold to the public. Topics include options, hedging, margin requirements, and the rules and regulations that govern them.

Municipal Securities Rulemaking Board

Until the mid-20th century the municipal bond industry operated by its own self-imposed rules and without any government oversight. Most bond customers were institutional—insurance companies, banks, pension funds—rather than individual investors. Things changed in the early 1970s, as new types of players entered the market. Individual buyers attracted to the tax-free feature gravitated towards these bonds, yet they were generally less knowledgeable than institutional buyers. At the same time there was a sharp growth in the numbers of dealers entering the market, yet the new entrants seem disinclined to "go by the old rules" of bond trading. The result was growing fraud and abuse, as well as a breakdown of longstanding industry standards. To address this problem Congress stepped in, creating the Municipal Securities Rulemaking Board (MSRB) in 1975. Its mandate was to develop standards and rules for institutions and persons involved in underwriting, trading, and selling municipal securities. Like FINRA, the MRSB is an SRO subject to the oversight of the SEC. Its members include securities firms, broker-dealers, and banks engaged in trading tax-exempt and taxable municipal bonds. However, the rules do not extend to issuers of municipal bonds, which are generally exempt from the legislation. In addition to municipal bonds (commonly known as "munis"), MRSB rules apply to 529 college education plans (a tax-advantaged savings plan earmarked for higher education expenses) and Build America Bonds (taxable bonds created by the 2009 American Recovery and Reinvestment Act). While the MRSB is mandated to develop investor protection rules, it does not have the power to enforce them. Its rules are enforced by other federal regulatory bodies, including the SEC, the Federal Reserve, and the Office of the Comptroller of the Currency.

In 2010 the MRSB was significantly restructured with the passage of the Dodd-Frank Act. The law extended MRSB's rulemaking authority to cover financial advisers who provide counsel to state and local governments and pension funds on municipal securities, municipal derivatives, and other investment issues. The MSRB now consists of both independent public members and representatives of municipal advisers.

The MRSB has an online electronic database for use by the general public. Launched in 2008 EMMA (Electronic Municipal Market Access system) contains disclosure documents that provide information about municipal bonds, notes, 529 college savings plans, and more. Included are official statements about new municipal bond offerings, refunding documents, and periodic disclosure documents, all of which provide material information about the bond issue. EMMA also offers price, yield, and interest rate data, as well as general educational material for bond investors.

North American Securities Administrators Association

The North American Securities Administrators Association (NASAA) is not a household name. In fact even people in the securities industry are often unfamiliar with it. It is an organization of securities market administrators from states, provinces, and territories in North America, including Mexico, the United States, and Canada. Members of the voluntary association are mandated to protect the public, educate the investing public, investigate violations of state or provincial securities' law, and carry out other enforcement functions. It encourages information sharing between members about common regulatory problems. Most importantly the NASAA oversees the licensing and testing of its members.

Despite its relatively low profile among the general public, the organization prides itself on its longstanding history in the securities industry. Founded in 1919, it has been around longer than any Federal regulatory body, predating the founding of the SEC by 15 years.

International Organization of Securities Commissions

In a world of interconnected financial systems, complex problems can arise. As a result regulatory bodies throughout the world have been forced to take a larger view. One step in that direction is the International Organization of Securities Commissions (IOSCO), an association of the national authorities that regulate the world's securities and futures markets. Its members are typically the main financial regulator from each country; thus, the SEC is the body that represents the United States. Originally a Pan-American association of securities commissions, it was created in 1974 to foster financial cooperation among North and South American exchanges. Gradually over the decades it outgrew its Pan-American focus and became an international body. By 1983 it had added securities regulators from France, the United Kingdom, Korea, and Indonesia to its membership roster. As of 2011 it had members from 95 percent of the world's securities markets.

Today IOSCO claims to be the international standard setter for securities markets, though like the United Nations its power is limited. Its primary role on the global stage is more as a cooperative forum and information exchange than as a true regulatory body with power over its members. Nevertheless it has adopted a comprehensive set of benchmarks for global securities markets, called the *Objectives and Principles of Securities Regulation* or, more informally, *the IOSCO Principles*. The 2008 investment debacle underscored the need for global cooperation to reduce the possibility of global collapse of the capital markets; with this in mind, IOSCO has developed new benchmarks for global cooperation, specifically a *Multilateral Memorandum of Understanding* designed to encourage transnational information exchange and cooperation. Today national regulators meet several times per year at the organization's permanent secretariat in Madrid or at other global locales.

Chapter 3

On the Job

You have studied hard for many years and now, your MBA is in hand. How should you start looking for a job? The first step is to decide what type of career you want. Do you want to work for yourself or someone else? Consider the options: you can work as an investment adviser with a brand-name wealth management firm, or start your own consultancy. You can follow a conventional asset management career at an established regional firm, or lay plans to start your own mutual fund one day. There is also the question of the corporate culture to which you are best suited. You can work for a major Wall Street firm, a regional second tier company, or a boutique firm tucked into a small town.

If managing money is your passion, but you are not ready to go it alone, you can start by doing research at an established company, work into a fund manager slot, and later, with experience under your belt, go independent. If you want to sell investments in some capacity, you have multiple options to choose from in investment banking, retail brokerage, and private equity. But while many people dream of working for themselves, entrepreneurship has many risks and perils, especially for the uninitiated. Rest assured that it is perfectly acceptable to start out at a traditional company, or even stay with them for one's entire career. Either path can offer rich financial rewards and a fulfilling lifelong career.

In this chapter, you will find investment job descriptions organized by functional category. This is only a small sampling of the many jobs available. In some cases, the jobs cut across several sectors. For example, the research analyst job is applicable to investment banking, private equity, retail brokerage, and others. You will also find that job duties overlap in the real world: for instance, a broker may also have advisory or sales duties. Finally, as you ponder your career path, consider the role that technologies of the future will have on your chosen profession. Automation is a two-edged sword: it is creates new jobs and eliminates others. It is best to avoid those jobs that have a foreseeable expiration date.

Advisory Services

There are a lot of different names for this job—financial planner, personal financial planner, personal financial adviser and financial consultant—but they all amount to about the same thing. They are a combination of adviser and salesman, offering their hybrid services to individual or retail customers. For our purposes here, we will refer to them here as personal financial advisers.

Institutional Relationship Manager

The institutional relationship manager, as its name suggests, works with the institutional clients of his firm, which is usually an asset management firm. *Institutional* can refer to corporations, pension plans, endowments, and even high net worth individuals. *High net worth* is generally defined as having a net worth of several million at the very least, though some firms put the floor much higher. Institutional relationship managers may function in several capacities: they may be advisers only, providing counseling services for a fee but not doing any product selling. Or they may serve an account manager role, working directly with the company's representative to resolve day-to-day issues. They may also dispense advice and counsel, offering solutions for the client's problems. The underlying objective of the role is to sell new services or products to the institutional client whenever possible. The job is not a junior position; it is generally held by middle to senior level professionals. Generally speaking, the institutional sector serves financially sophisticated clientele. As such, firms in this industry tend to look for high-caliber and multi-degreed people with a noteworthy background. To be considered, you must have superior credentials, including an MBA from a reputable university and one or more certifications. With these higher requirements come higher salaries than you will find on the retail side of the business. Higher salaries, of course, mean greater competition for available slots. But stellar résumés alone won't always suffice to land you an interview. To put yourself on the radar screen of key decision makers, use networking, consulting and old-fashioned persistence.

Personal Financial Adviser

The personal financial adviser job entails counseling individuals on various aspects of their personal finances, including choice of investments, portfolio strategy, savings, insurance, estate planning, college funding, retirement, and taxes. Based on the client's needs, the personal financial adviser will develop a detailed financial strategy. Some advisers specialize in only one type of advice, such as retirement planning, although most counsel individuals on the full range of their financial needs. The advisers' compensation could be derived from commissions on sales of financial products, fees based on assets under management, fixed fees, hourly fees or a combination of these. Some of the terms are similar enough to be thoroughly confusing. The term "fee-only" refers to charging fees derived only from the client, which excludes things like commissions, referral fees, and finder's fees. "Fee-based" means that the fee is derived from a mix of client-paid fees (fixed, hourly, asset-based) and commissions. Suffice it to say that personal financial advisers generally use fee-based or commission forms of compensation.

Another genre in this category is one who provides strategic advice only, charging an hourly or fixed fee for their professional services and earning no commissions or referral fees. Most of them call themselves *financial planners* and often hold a certification (like the CFP(r) or CFA(r)) to distinguish themselves from the garden-variety salesman/adviser. They deal with the big picture, counseling the client on issues that will affect his entire financial life for years or decades to come. There is definitely a market for this type of adviser. Some clients see a conflict of interest in advisers who make commissions on the products they sell, and will only work with the advice-only type.

Full-service advisers analyze all aspects of a person's financial situation and draw up a comprehensive financial plan for them to follow. The job demands extensive client interface, meticulous follow-up, and superior customer service. If the adviser succeeds, then the relationship may develop into a lucrative, long-term one lasting decades. Like stockbrokers, personal financial advisers must find their own clients through cold calling, referrals, networking, and other standard business development techniques. This requires an entrepreneurial personality adept at finding and maintaining a customer base. People who have a well-developed social network will be in the strongest competitive position. It helps to come from a sales background because strong interpersonal skills are critical in this customer-facing profession. If you have previously worked as a stockbroker, insurance salesperson, or as any type of sales agent, your people skills will no doubt come in handy.

Since the primary daily interface is with clients and not supervisory types, the job lends itself well to self-employment. For this reason, at least 40 percent of the personal financial advisers in the United States are self-employed, running small investment advisory firms. If you plan to sell stocks, bonds, mutual funds, or other securities to clients, then you are required to have a securities license (e.g., Series 6, 7, or 63), which will require sponsorship by a FINRA member firm. If your goal is to start your own advisory firm, bear in mind that you must first work for an established firm while getting your licenses. Additionally, you must register with either the SEC or the state securities authority where your business is located. The general rule of thumb is that advisers who manage $25 million or more in assets must register with the SEC. Those managing less than $25 million must register with the state commission. Once you are successfully registered, you become a Registered Investment Adviser or RIA. As previously noted, it improves your credentials to be either chartered or certified.

Wealth Relationship Manager

This is another job that goes by many different names. Private banker, private client services manager, wealth relationship manager, and high net worth adviser are a few of the common titles given to the adviser who serves a wealthy clientele. We will use the term

Fast Facts

Jules, We Hardly Knew Ye

Paul Erdman was not the first financier to pick up the pen. Long before Jules Verne became a genre-smashing science fiction writer, he was a stockbroker. It is not clear why the rebellious writer made such an unlikely career choice. Perhaps his engagement to a young woman named Honorine de Viane pushed him to it, or maybe it was because his father had cut off all financial support. Either way, the money Verne made from trading securities helped him launch his science fiction career. He rose daily at the crack of dawn, putting in five hours of fiction writing before arriving at the Paris Bourse as the bell struck 10 A.M. This abstemious schedule led to his first novel, *Five Weeks in a Balloon*.

But the young financier did not seem to have his heart in it. In fact the most important day of his stockbroker career was the day he left it. As the apocryphal tale goes, Verne stood on the steps of the Paris Exchange, shouting to his fellow brokers as he waved his new publishing contract, "I've just written a new kind of novel, and if it succeeds, it will be a gold mine. I'll write books while you are buying stocks. And let's see who makes the most money!"

Is Jules Verne's story one worthy of emulation for future stockbrokers? Hardly. But it does remind us that the stockbroker profession can be the launching pad for many a splendid career.

"wealth relationship manager" here. These managers serve the high net worth market, although the definition of "high net worth" varies by institution, ranging from as low as one million to as high as $50 million as the starting point for entry into this exclusive group. Some firms define the higher echelon group as "ultra high net worth". Wealth relationship managers work for brokerage firms, banks, and asset management firms, and typically sell the products they are recommending. They may also perform financial management tasks for the client, ranging from choosing investments, to managing estate plans, to authorizing payments, to writing checks on the client's behalf.

Wealth management firms often charge high net worth clients a fee based on the percentage of assets under management. Given how large these pools of assets often are, this can amount to a huge pile of income for the wealth manager and his or her firm. Like stockbrokers, wealth managers must find and maintain their own client base. This means going where their clients go, whether at jet-set enclaves, social clubs, or at other venues favored by elite groups. Not surprisingly, wealth managers often find themselves following the same affluent lifestyle as their clients. With its promise of a high income and posh standard of living, the career has high barriers to entry. Competition is fierce, and it is a buyer's market in terms of talent. An MBA is almost essential and a few licenses will be needed; in most cases, a Series 7 and 63. Moreover, this is not a career for beginners. Its starting point is invariably at mid-career and almost never at entry level. Five to 10 years of experience in another wealth management role is mandatory. People who have other professional degrees, such as a law degree or medical degree, will have a hiring advantage. Since estate planning services are often needed by the wealthy, law degrees can help in understanding the contractual side of documents relevant to asset distribution and transfer. Well-connected people always have an edge in this business, but nothing is impossible for a determined and ambitious person, even one with less than sterling connections.

Asset Management

The term *asset management* is used in different ways in the industry, sometimes referring only to collective investment schemes (mutual funds, exchange-traded funds), while other times referring to any type of fund management (like private banking or wealth management), either institutional or individual. Here we are describing it mainly in the context of mutual and exchange traded funds. The upcoming section on Personal Advisers will consider private banking and wealth management activities.

Compliance Officer

Compliance officers are found throughout the finance industry. They are a security firm's internal watchdogs, responsible for overseeing its legal and regulatory practices. It must ensure that the firm is in full compliance with federal and state regulatory authorities. Compliance officers deal with any issue that touches on an industry regulation. They must ensure that an information blackout (known as the "Chinese wall") exists between any two departments that may have a conflict of interest in the SEC's eyes. They must monitor marketing communications to ensure that no insider information is being leaked and that communications do not engage in false advertising. Additionally officers must ensure that no employee is trading in *gray list securities*, periodically monitor the firm's information exchange with sister firms, and generally develop and implement the firm's ethical standards, policies, and procedures. Compliance officers typically work with internal and external attorneys and members of the securities commissions. A common career path is to start as an analyst, then move into senior management, and finally, into the compliance officer role.

Institutional Sales Manager

The duty of an institutional sales manager is to sell the firm's funds to institutional clients; e.g., pension funds, endowments, and banks. The job is travel-intensive, requiring ongoing visits to client offices, conferences, exhibits, and shows. The travel commitment can be as high as 50 percent of managers' time, and when they are not in airports, managers will probably find themselves working the phone or Internet for prospects. The manager is usually assigned to work a specific geographic territory, and if that territory is in an area without local offices of his firm, then he may even work out of his home. This requires a special type of person, one who can work independently, often in hotels, and without day-to-day contact with colleagues and subordinates. As with a stockbroker, a sales manager must mine his or her own territory for new clients, and that means round-the-clock cold calling and networking. Sales managers usually have to meet a target goal each month or quarter, such as 10 sales or 10 promising leads. On the other hand some firms use the sales manager only for high-level contacts or managerial duties, while using telemarketers to handle the bulk of the cold calling. Either way the job of institutional sales manager is not an entry-level job. It is a high level sales position involving in-depth knowledge of the fund products being sold. For this reason most sales managers start out as analysts or traders. It requires a minimum of an undergraduate degree, but an MBA is preferred. Series 7 and 63 licenses are generally required.

Portfolio Manager

Portfolio managers are responsible for overseeing the investments that go into mutual, exchange-traded, or closed-end funds. Using research reports and knowledge of the markets, they choose the securities that go into the fund's portfolio. They also monitor day-to-day trading activity and act as senior investment advisers for the firm as a whole. They typically have a staff of their own to supervise: research assistants, analysts, and the junior portfolio manager. The support staff will gather corporate and market intelligence for his review; he will then make the final decision on the security. Overall, the manager's most important task is to ensure that the trades are consistent with the fund's investment strategy. In the final analysis it is the portfolio manager who will be responsible, for better or worse, for the performance of the fund, and his compensation and advancement in the firm will depend on his track record in managing the fund.

When a fund performs well, its portfolio manager may achieve the renown of a rock star, attracting investors like a magnet. It is common for these managers to garner widespread media attention and to be featured on the cover of major investment magazines and newspapers. Their opinions and theories will be held in high esteem and investors will hang on their every word, in the hope that following their advice will allow them to achieve the manager's results. While very few portfolio managers achieve such guru stature, there is no doubt that their performance will be scrutinized closely by investors. All in all it takes many years of experience to achieve the skill necessary to manage a fund. You should count on *serving time* in research analyst and junior management roles before being given the opportunity to manage large sums of money. Many portfolio managers serve many years in the junior portfolio manager role before taking on the top job. Naturally, one or more securities licenses will be required.

Working for a mutual fund in any managerial role requires a certain type of personality. First and foremost, the job requires someone with an analytic and strategic bent. Second, a team spirit is a highly valued attribute. The job of portfolio manager—or any job in the asset management industry for that matter—is not well suited for loners and free spirits. Those with me-generation credos might also be ill-suited for the asset management world. (Finance does have a role for them—perhaps in brokerage or trading—just not here.) Those who fare well in the fund industry will have superior diplomatic, interpersonal, and group interaction skills. If you harbor prima donna instincts deep down in your soul but still want to work in asset management, it is best to keep them hidden while accumulating your portfolio management experience. Your advancement through the ranks will depend on your ability to convince your supervisors that your only goal is to help the team succeed. Yet corporate cultures differ by employer and region of the country. Each firm will have different degrees of expectation as to cultural conformity and independence of action. To find out how you might fit in, research the culture of your target employer. It may also help to talk to its current employees, if you know any, or to broach questions to the recruiter at a job interview.

Competition is fierce in the asset management industry. That is because there are a huge number of other funds available these days, a phenomenon that puts extreme pressure on individual funds to succeed. Managers must either perform or perish, so to speak, a very large ultimatum indeed. And given the element of chance in the securities markets, even the smartest and most diligent manager can put in a poor performance in certain markets. Nevertheless there are rich financial rewards for those who can deal with this level of performance pressure and that can amount to the millions of dollars per year for top performers.

Financial Analysis

Most investments start with research. To understand the potential profitability of a venture or company, an investment firm will need to do extensive due diligence. Research analysts are charged with this task, and they are found in almost every type of investment firm. Here are a few of the most common job titles.

Buy-Side Research Analyst

There are two types of analysts, buy-side and sell-side. The distinction is important because the two jobs require two different skill sets and two different types of people. The difference between the two is defined by the type of firm for which they work. Buy-side analysts may work for pension funds or mutual fund companies. Their research output is provided solely to their firm's own fund managers, and is not available for public consumption. Generally, they maintain a nonpublic, low profile. Since their research output is exclusive to their firm, buy-side analysts do not appear in the media touting their findings. The research is kept private because it is hoped that their findings will give the firm a competitive edge over other investors. Common daily tasks include talking to analysts at credit rating agencies or to sell-side analysts from brokerage firms. The role typically requires an MBA in finance, a Chartered Financial Analyst designation or the willingness to get one in the future, and strong quantitative skills. As with any analyst, a buy-side analyst's advancement in the firm is based on how accurate his forecasts are and whether his findings lead to healthy returns on investments for the firm.

Junior Research Analyst

For those without the credentials or education to enter as a full-fledged analyst, the junior analyst post is a good point of entry. For applicants with MBA study in progress, or even for a career switcher coming from a non-financial background, the job is a great way to get experience in the research process. The junior analyst will serve as an assistant to one analyst or a group of analysts. Tasks include reading financial statements and annual reports, maintaining computer databases, analyzing external research, synthesizing research, and editing and proofreading the analysts' work. Expect to be assigned lots of mind-numbing grunt work that no one else wants to do. Your political stature within the firm will fall somewhere between an ant and a cockroach on the totem pole, and you may even be the target of pranks and tomfoolery by second year analysts. But do not let it get to you. Dust yourself off and show them you can take it in stride. Use this initiation period to get yourself noticed by the firm's top brass. The job will put you right in the path of the top people in the research department, including the director and fund managers. It is expected that a junior analyst is in training to move up the ladder, first to the analyst role, then to a senior analyst spot, and eventually to a directorate position. Junior analysts are hired right out of undergraduate or graduate school, although a couple of years experience elsewhere is commonly found on applicants' résumés.

Research Analyst: General

In an asset management firm, analysts generate research for the use of fund managers. This usually involves both quantitative and qualitative analysis of every aspect of the target investment, from poring over annual reports and financial statements to doing economic, regulatory, market, and industry analysis. Research analysts must provide the fund manager with a buy, sell, or hold recommendation, and may also be required to brainstorm ideas for new investments. But while analysts support a fund manager, they do not necessarily report to him or her; instead, they usually report to a director within the research department.

Research analysts also do competitive analysis of the target, look at political and regulatory issues, and assess its management expertise. While analysts in boutique firms will be generalists, those in large firms tend to specialize in an industry sector such as food service or oil and gas, or in a region such as Latin America or Emerging Market. In any event entry-level analysts should expect to spend many hours at their desk with only their calculator and computer for company. Top-tier accounting and financial skills are paramount, as there is considerable number crunching involved in the job. The chartered financial analyst designation is a good thing to have and may even be required by some employers.

Research analysts are found in just about every type of financial industry sector, including brokerages, investment banks, private equity firms, and asset management companies. The position is usually a stepping-stone to more lucrative jobs in portfolio management, brokerage, or mergers and acquisitions, though it does not have to be. Some people prefer to spend their entire career as an analyst, and there is nothing wrong with that. Depending on your degree of comfort with computer programs, you can choose to be either a fundamentals analyst or a quantitative analyst (also known as *quant*). Fundamentals analysts make recommendations based on their own general review of the company's financials (the future direction of profits, revenue, debt, and other basics) and management quality. Quants, on the other hand, must have advanced mathematical and computer skills, as they will use complex software programs to perform the analysis. You do not need a Ph.D., but it is surprising how many quants have one, so to be competitive in the job market, it is not a bad idea to get one. Quantitative analysts develop computer models used in securities valuation and program trading. In addition to advanced mathematical training, the position requires mastery of programming languages, computer proficiency, and an analytic orientation. Good communication skills are valuable too, as there are client-facing tasks involved in the role. Surprisingly, you do not

Everyone

Knows

Financial Certifications

In today's competitive market having one or more financial certifications is vitally important. Earning the certification, however, is not an easy process. To pass the exam, most certifications require intensive study and a high level of expertise in the field. Here is a short list of some common certifications and charters available to financial professionals:

Certified Financial Planner(r) (CFP(r)): CFP certification is for those who need to demonstrate expertise in advisory and planning services. The certificate means that you have competency in the financial planning field. You must pass a test on many financial topics, including stocks, bonds, retirement planning, taxes, and estate planning. The program is administered by the Certified Financial Planner Board of Standards (http://www.cfp.net). Candidates must also have qualifying work experience and are bound to follow the Board's code of ethics and professional standards of conduct.

Chartered Financial Analyst(r) (CFA(r)): This designation is administered by The CFA Institute (http://www.cfainstitute.org). To obtain the CFA charter, you must have three years of qualifying work experience and pass several rigorous examinations that test your knowledge of accounting, economics, security analysis, and professional standards.

necessarily need financial training for the job. If you can present superior mathematical and computer expertise, the firm will likely train you in the basics of portfolio theory and valuation.

Research analysts put in plenty of hours at the computer screen, but the job is by no means a pure desk job. As you become more seasoned, your duties may include visiting companies and having heavy telephone contact with executives, investors, and other top-tier industry pros. Analysts spend a lot of time at airports en route to visit the target's headquarters or facilities. The job will also allow you ample interface with your own firm's senior managers, and thus has great political advantages. Furthermore your final recommendation on the security or company is a critical component of the firm's

Certified Fund Specialist(r) (CFS(r)): A Certified Funds Specialist is appropriate for professionals in the mutual funds industry, typically those who want to advise clients on funds. The certification shows that the holder has expertise in all relevant areas of the funds industry, including portfolio theory, annuities, income tax issues, and estate planning, to name a few. It is granted by the Institute of Business and Finance (http://www.icfs.com), which provides training and testing services for candidates.

Certified Government Financial Manager (CGFM): This certification is for individuals seeking to work at the local, state, or federal level in government regulation and accountability. It is offered by the Association of Government Accountants (AGA), which serves the profession by holding conferences and seminars, and through publication of periodicals and educational materials. The AGA also offers other certifications.

Chartered Financial Consultant(r) (ChFC(r)): This charter is for those interested in a career as a personal investment adviser or financial planner. It is administered by The American College (http://www.theamericancollege.edu). Individuals holding the charter have demonstrated their comprehensive knowledge of financial planning, including retirement planning, tax issues, investment, insurance and estate planning. Qualifying work experience is also required.

decision-making process. Senior partners or managers will scrutinize your work closely and base investments on your analyses. In the end, your weeks of research will come down to one of three words: *buy* or *sell* or *hold*. Hopefully, your research will lead to the right investment decision, and if it does, your stature within the firm will grow. This makes the job a valuable stepping-stone to other opportunities.

Although a freshly minted MBA or even a bachelor's degree in business will get you hired at many firms, it is even better if you can present an industry specialty. Candidates who combine a business degree with certain types of industry experience (e.g., transportation, oil and gas, scientific instruments) also increase their odds of being hired. Having a relevant internship on the résumé is helpful too. The ability to present an MBA with a master's or doctoral degree in another field (e.g., chemistry, environmental science, medicine) will surely put you at the top of the list. And for analyst jobs in high technology, nothing is more attractive to recruiters than a candidate with an engineering degree and/or a high technology background.

Recruiters pay a great deal of attention to MBA graduates because companies like to indoctrinate candidates from the earliest stage of their careers. Even so, they are still open—even eager in some cases—to hiring mid-career candidates for some analyst positions. Seasoned candidates—and this includes people switching from an entirely different field—can offer valuable subject matter expertise not found in the standard MBA analyst. It all depends on what the career switcher candidate can bring to the table. An airline pilot with transportation industry knowledge or a biochemist with pharmaceutical expertise will have obvious advantages for firms aiming to invest in those industries, and they will often pay a premium for people with this knowledge. The key to making this career strategy work for you is to apply at companies with investment objectives that closely match your own expertise.

Whether you are a mid-career switcher or a recent graduate, for an analyst position at a private or venture capital firm it is advisable to present an advanced degree of some sort. Most venture capitalists have advanced degrees, although it is not impossible to get hired with just an undergraduate degree. A possible career path for the undergraduate applicant is to work as an analyst for several years, and then return to college for an MBA. However, a promising candidate with only rudimentary credentials can still attract interest if he or she has *the right stuff* and can prove it in a knock-it-out-of-the-ballpark interview: demonstrating outstanding presentation skills, a flawless knowledge of the industry, and a persuasive explanation of why you want to work in venture or private capital.

Research Assistant

The research assistant job is usually held by those who do not have the qualifications to be a junior research analyst, due to insufficient academic training or experience. An example of this would be a recent baccalaureate in the humanities who does not yet have the required quantitative skills. The assistant may be working on a graduate degree or taking math and finance courses in the evening. Like the junior analyst job, the research assistant job is often held by people who are using it as a kind of internship, hoping to get expo-sure to the business. It is not the best way to get your foot in the door (better to start as a junior analyst), but necessary for some. When the degree or coursework is complete, the individual will usually move into a junior analyst's chair. If you do not qualify for an analyst's job yet, this is a reasonable way to gain entry into the field. Job duties can range from basic spreadsheet work to gathering information on the target prospect to purely administrative tasks.

Sell-Side Research Analyst

Sell-side analysts are often seen on financial cable shows pontificat-ing on trends in stocks and markets. These high-profile financial forecasters typically work for brokerage firms or companies that manage individual accounts. Unlike buy-side analysts who gener-ate proprietary research, the sell-side analyst generates research for public consumption. Not all of them become household names or television personalities, though that is one possible career path for analysts who love the limelight. More commonly they will publish their findings in newsletters, give interviews, appear at conferences, give speeches, or use whatever means are available to showcase their research. Others will simply provide clients of their own firm with buy or sell recommendations. By helping investors reach a decision on a particular security, the brokerage benefits because it receives a commission with every trade the client makes.

Other common tasks for sell-side analysts include participating in analyst teleconferences with target company executives, meeting in person with those executives, and touring their offices, plants, and facilities. All this is done to gauge the value of the security in question. Broad industry, political, and economic analyses can be equally important pieces of the investment puzzle, so sell-side ana-lyst's reports will frequently include this type of research. As you might expect, the job requires an articulate and polished professional with good presentation skills. Strong quantitative skills, a chartered financial analyst designation or the commitment to work towards it, and an MBA are also important background qualifications.

Government Regulation

There has never been a better time to enter a career in government regulation. In fact, the opportunities are so rich that even mid-career professionals might want to consider a switch to the public sector. In response to the Dodd-Frank Act of 2010, federal agencies have restructured and augmented their employee base. As far as the SEC is concerned, it plans to increase its staff levels by about 10 percent, which means about 375 new hires in the early part of the decade. But given the added oversight duties facing the SEC, this may be just the beginning. It present and future staffing needs are discussed by SEC Chairman Mary L. Schapiro in this excerpt from her March 10, 2011, Congressional testimony before the Subcommittee on Securities, Insurance, and Investment:

> In addition to carrying out our longstanding core responsibilities, last year's enactment of the Dodd-Frank Act has added significantly to the SEC's workload. In the short term, it requires the agency to promulgate more than 100 new rules, create five new offices, and produce more than 20 studies and reports. The law assigns the SEC considerable new responsibilities that will have a significant long-term impact on the agency's workload, including oversight of the over-the-counter (OTC) derivatives market and hedge fund advisers; registration of municipal advisers and security-based swap market participants; enhanced supervision of nationally recognized statistical rating organizations (NRSROs) and clearing agencies; heightened regulation of asset-backed securities (ABS); and creation of a new whistleblower program.

She then explains some of the recent staffing and hiring changes that have transpired since the Dodd-Frank Act:

> Without a doubt, the most critical element to our success in improving the Commission's operations is the agency's talented staff. Over the past two years, we have installed new management across the major divisions and offices of the Commission. These new senior managers are playing a vital role in our efforts to transform the agency. During my first year, we brought in new leadership to run the four largest operating units-the Division of Enforcement, the Office of Compliance Inspections and Examinations (OCIE), the Division of Corporation Finance, and the Division of Trading and Markets. We also created a new Division of Risk, Strategy, and Financial Innovation to re-focus the agency's attention on—and response to—new products, trading practices, and risks... At all levels we have focused on hiring individuals with key skill sets that reflect the rapidly changing markets under our supervision.

The presentation suggests the sheer growth and dynamism of the agency, as well as the many attendant opportunities for candidates. While we cannot discuss all the jobs alluded to by Ms. Schapiro, here are three of the most common ones.

Regulatory Accountants

Regulatory accountants work at both the federal and state levels. At the federal level their primary task is to audit the financial statements and public disclosures filed by companies and exchanges. If they find irregularities or if the filings do not meet SEC standards, then they must launch a larger investigation. The work may take the accountant into controversial and difficult areas of accounting and auditing theory. Once an investigation is launched, the accountant will become a key member of the investigatory team reviewing the case and will have significant interface with other internal accountants, as well as attorneys, securities experts, and financial consultants. The accountant may participate in interviews and depositions, and may have interface with civil and criminal investigators. Regulatory accountants have extensive contact with the target company, including its attorneys and corporate officers. Other public duties include written communications with members of the public who file complaints or write letters on a variety of topics. The accountants may also be involved in amending and updating accounting rules.

Creativity and high intelligence are essential qualities to bring to the table, as much of the work involves dealing with new, untested, or unusual accounting methods. The SEC typically hires experienced accountants for the middle-tier and senior regulatory accountant positions. The most desirable candidates are Certified Public Accountants with three to eight years of public accounting experience related to the securities industry.

Securities Compliance Examiner

A securities examiner sees a slice of the finance industry that the private sector never sees. By studying the financial documents of hundreds of companies, they have a bird's-eye view of the American securities system. Their task is to ensure that no securities laws have been violated, and that the firm's compliance controls are adequate. The job has a broad and challenging range of duties and

Keeping in Touch

Foreign Languages: Bridging the Global Communication Gap

Good communication skills are essential for effective dealings in the securities industry. But communication may be hampered when the two parties speak different languages. All the more reason for securities firms to hire people with fluency in foreign languages. Candidates who are conversant in multiple languages, especially Chinese, Japanese, and South Asian languages, will be especially sought after. Having a background in a foreign culture, including knowledge of its business practices and social etiquette, will also be prized attributes. It does not matter whether the knowledge is acquired from academia or personal experience; in fact, people with foreign living experience may rate higher with recruiters than a person with a cultural studies degree. Whether you plan to work abroad or just communicate by email with foreign counterparts, you will find that international communication skills will pay big dividends throughout your career.

responsibilities. Compliance examiners spend their days poring over financial statements of firms, companies and exchanges. They may perform background research and review the firm's records and operations. One day may find them reviewing a mutual fund portfolio; another day, a broker-dealer's sales activities; and on still another day, the financials of a multinational financial giant. Some jobs only require examiners to do deskwork, while others require travel to companies for on-site inspections. Travel is usually within the examiner's base city, region, or district. Some of their cases will involve minor, commonplace violations, while others may evolve into massive investigations involving intricate new areas of accounting theory and the titanic downfall of a major player. Such cases may necessitate high-profile legal proceedings and become newsmakers.

Securities laws and regulations are highly complex and take many years to master. Those who do achieve mastery of these laws can become highly valued players. Their experience and knowledge can be taken to the private sector for a lucrative second career.

Many government regulators use the job as a stepping-stone for a second-act career with an industry player. Becoming an examiner is perhaps the best way to learn securities regulations. In the United States securities examiner jobs can be found in the eleven regional offices of the SEC, as well as at the Washington, D.C., headquarters.

In the aftermath of the last decade's financial scandals, the SEC has reorganized its national examination program, including the training and recruitment practices of its examiners. This augurs well for hiring in this area. The program has been fortified and enhanced, resulting in the need for examiners with special training and skills consistent with the firm they are examining. This suggests that a private sector energy analyst or even someone with direct industry experience in addition to financial skills would be in a strong position for an SEC examiner job.

State Regulators

If you are interested in a career as a state regulator, there are 50 different regulatory frameworks to consider, plus those in U.S. territories and Canada. Some state regulators fall under the Secretary of State's office, others under the state's Department of Commerce, and still others under a separate Securities Board or Commission. Review the list below to find out how to contact the state authority in which you are interested. While we cannot list all the possible jobs here, as one example, here is a brief review of some of the jobs carried out by the Securities Board of the state of Texas.

Enforcement Staff

The Texas State Securities Board enforces the Texas Securities Act. Its enforcement staff is involved in the detection and prevention of violations of the Act. Enforcement staff may recommend that a case be submitted to the Texas Securities Commissioner for sanction. Among the acts that may lead to sanction are illegal sales of unregistered nonexempt securities, sales of securities by unregistered dealers, and fraud committed in connection with the sale of securities. If the enforcement officer suspects a violation of the Act, he or she has the authority to recommend that a matter be referred to the Attorney General for criminal prosecution of the company, or that other legal actions be taken.

Inspections and Compliance Staff

The Texas State Securities Board hires inspections and compliance staff to check up on the business premises of persons and firms registered with the Texas Securities Commissioner. They must ensure that the registrant is in compliance with all Texas securities laws and regulations. Compliance officers usually show up unannounced to do on-site inspections. Any registered firm or dealer in the state of Texas that is not a member of FINRA is subject to having its operations inspected. The focus is on registered investment advisers and other non-FINRA registered dealers located in Texas. Compliance staff is also mandated to review and investigate complaints made by the general public. They may also review financial statements and other disclosures by Texas registered dealers.

Trading and Brokerage Services

Trading and brokerage services make up a large part of the finance industry. Below are overviews of some key positions.

Commodity Broker

Commodity brokers do about the same thing as stockbrokers, except they trade in a different asset: commodities rather than equity. These brokers buy and sell the futures contracts on behalf of their clients or their firms' clients. The client is usually a large company that uses the product in the manufacturing or production process, but it can also be a speculator, either individual or institutional. Many commodity brokers start out as stockbrokers, since it is easier to enter the equity trading business. Commodity brokers are a much smaller and elite group of people, typically numbering in the 60,000 range, compared to nearly 700,000 for stockbrokers in the United States. For the limited number of jobs available, the profession is highly competitive.

Commodity brokers engage in several types of activities. They can be floor traders, commodity trading advisers, or commodity pool operators. Floor traders execute commodity orders on the floor of the exchange, while trading advisers counsel clients on commodities. A commodity pool is the commodities equivalent of a mutual fund; the commodities pool operator puts investors' money into a collective and manages the funds on their behalf. This job involves executing trades on behalf of clients as well as giving them advice. The compensation structure for commodity brokers is usually commission-based. Like stockbrokers, commodity brokers must constantly

be on the lookout for new customers and accounts since their liveli-
hoods depend on the size of their client base.

Desk Trader

The job of a desk trader is not quite as high-pressure as are other trader
jobs. Working at brokerages, these traders take and place orders on
behalf of the firms' clients. Desk traders do not give advice or help the
client make a decision; they are just order takers who know how to
execute trades. This is the person to whom a retail investor will speak
when he or she places an order to buy or sell a security with a brokerage firm. The desk trader job got its start with the advent of virtual
stock markets like Nasdaq and the O.T.C. in the last century. Traders
bought and sold stocks, first by phone and later by Internet. Later, as
other stock markets automated, their role expanded.

Prospective desk traders can expect their daily companions to
be a computer screen and a smart phone. Human interface will be
largely limited to very brief contact with clients, internal managers,
and the buyer/seller. They spend a lot of their time on the phone—
usually several at once—in a mad dash to find a buyer or seller
for the requested trade. Desk traders are limited to trading for the
firm's clients; they are not allowed to place orders for the firm's own
account or for their own account. As the job title implies, it is pretty
much *a desk job*. Job performance is based on how efficiently and
accurately they execute trades. Although the post may sound almost
administrative, it is not: the job requires a thorough knowledge of
markets and finance and an SEC securities license.

Floor Broker

Floor brokers, sometimes known as pit brokers, also work on the
floor of the exchange, but are employed by a member firm. They
execute trades on behalf of the firm's clients, as opposed to floor
traders, who trade for their own account. When a firm or investor
wishes to buy or sell a security, the firm's own traders will dispatch
the order through their firm's computers to the broker on the floor of
the exchange. The floor broker will proceed to negotiate a good price
with other floor brokers representing other firms. If an agreement
is reached as to price, the order will be placed, and confirmation of
the transaction will be sent back to the firm's in-house trader. Their
compensation is usually commission-based. This job, like any job on

the floor of the exchange, is highly volatile, requiring an adrenalin-fueled personality who thrives in the loud and often tumultuous atmosphere of the floor. Nevertheless floor brokers need only work during the hours the exchange is open, which mean that they will need to put in fewer hours than stockbrokers or investment bankers. For some the relatively short but hyper-intense work schedule is the ideal work environment. Like any exchange job, floor brokers must meet the exchange's requirements, including having a securities license.

Floor Trader

A floor trader, also called an *individual liquidity provider,* is a member of a stock or other securities exchange who trades solely for his own account. The name derives from the fact that the trader has a physical presence on the trading floor. Even today these traders use the open outcry method of placing trades, racing around the exchange floor to find buyers willing to buy at a certain price specified by the seller. As prices change quickly in a turbulent market, traders are under constant pressure to execute deals at the specified price. If buyers could not find sellers and sellers could not find buyers, the market might well grind to a halt. So floor traders perform a valuable service for the whole exchange. Essentially, they are matchmakers, providing liquidity to the market by matching sellers and buyers. This is another high-pressure career requiring high energy, nerves of steel, and given the large amounts of money at stake, intestinal fortitude of the highest magnitude. Yet this may not be the smartest career track to pursue in the future. As automated trading systems become more and more entrenched, the classical floor trader's job may be put on the endangered species list. Interested people should track the industry developments to see whether computers usurp this role, or whether the old-fashioned trader will continue to be needed for certain tasks.

Retail Stockbroker

Stockbrokers, also known as *account executives* or *registered representatives*, are essentially technically trained salespeople. They must have all the skills that make for an effective seller, and these include communication skills, people skills, persuasiveness, high motivation, and an independent streak. Stockbrokers must be highly knowledgeable in all the investments products they plan to sell. To be competitive in this job market, a college degree with coursework in finance and business is essential. To enter the trade, you must pass one or more of the FINRA exams, including the Series 7 Examination, which will test you on a wide range of financial topics and SEC rules and regulations. As with any investment job, a background check is required. In addition to the Series 7, some states require aspiring stockbrokers to pass the Series 63 Examination. This examination covers the principles of state securities regulation reflected in the Uniform Securities Act. However, many brokerage firms will hire people without these licenses as long as the candidate takes the exams at a later date. Firms may also help aspiring licensees by paying for training and classes, a practice referred to as sponsoring. While working on a license, new recruits may work as trading assistants, supporting established brokers with tasks like cold calling, administrative tasks, and "gopher" work. Or they may apprentice by working as a paid or unpaid intern.

Stockbrokers have extensive interaction with clients and prospective clients. Since they must find their own customers, they must be highly energetic and able to withstand a fast-paced, high-pressure, and unstructured environment. Long hours are common, and there is rarely time for coffee breaks or shopping on your lunch break. Work days are structured around the times the securities markets are open: for West Coast brokers, this means starting at 6 A.M. But the job has its perks: some of those long hours can be spent schmoozing with potential clients at resorts, restaurants, or bars. As with any customer-contact job, personal appearance is a critical factor. Clothing and image will affect the broker's success, for better or for worse, fair or unfair. Although entry-level brokers will usually get a small base stipend to live on while they develop a client base, established brokers work solely on commission.

Much of a new stockbroker's time will be taken up in prospecting activities like cold calling, networking, or passing out business cards at social events. As a result they spend most of their time as independent operators, interfacing more with clients than with members of their own firm. They must be able to work with little or no supervision, although some brokerages will sponsor office competitions to motivate brokers to meet targets. Opportunities for interaction with senior management are limited, especially at the larger brokerage houses. Bottom-line performance is the best if not only way to move up the career ladder, and those who do not meet sales targets will quickly be out of a job. Truly, this is a *sell* or *perish* type job, though this does not mean that you should whip up sales for sales sake to the detriment of your clients. Securities transactions must be appropriate and within legal guidelines. Excessive buying and selling of securities without regard to the client's investment objectives is called *churning*, and it is a violation of SEC Rule 15c1-7 and other securities laws.

Trader

Traders are very similar in some ways to brokers and quite different in others. Like brokers, they buy and sell securities and work in a pressure cooker environment. The difference is that they execute trades based on the instructions of a portfolio manager, rather than by request of retail, institutional, or other external clients. Typically they work at large investment management firms and trade stocks, funds, bonds, currencies, options, futures, or securities underwritten by that firm. Their trades are usually transacted with commercial banks, other investment banks, and large institutional investors. The core task of a trader is to execute buy and sell orders at the behest of the portfolio manager, who will usually specify a price point for the transaction. Traders must stay constantly on top of market prices and events affecting the securities markets. Their daily grind will consist of poring over analyst reports and mass media publications to keep up with the latest developments that could affect price trends. Clearly, this is a fast paced job that will leave little time for leisurely coffee breaks.

But unlike brokers, traders have no contact with the public and do no selling. Thus all those skills needed by brokers, such as people skills and salesmanship, are irrelevant to the trader job. (Though do not throw out your Emily Post quite yet—to navigate the treacherous terrain of office politics, you may need some social skills.) Instead, their primary daily interface will be with a computer screen, and they must be comfortable working independently. Their focus is on the securities they are responsible for trading, and they will be judged on their ability to achieve the best possible prices for their firm. Some traders choose to remain in this role throughout their career, while for others the trader job is only one step on the path to portfolio manager. Because of its high-energy demands, the post tends to be the most attractive to younger people, who will move to less frenetic jobs as they mellow out and mature. One does not typically get hired as a trader right out of college; instead, one works up to this position.

Since trading can be extremely turbulent, the job requires a certain type of personality. Perhaps a good way to describe it would be a classical type-A personality who thrives on stress and feverish activity. The post also requires a shrewd understanding of market dynamics, technical expertise in the products you will be selling, as well as a grasp of how human behavior and psychology can shape market trends. Even though people skills are not really needed (except as a survival skill for office politics) in this job, the ability to understand the behavior of other large traders is essential. Those eyeing a career in derivatives or options trading should have a technical degree like engineering or math.

Chapter 4

Tips for Success

Every person about to embark on an investment career should ask themselves the simple question—*why do I want to work in the finance industry?* Not only will you be asked this by relatives and friends alike in the course of your personal life, but the question will be repeatedly posed to you at job interviews. The answer may seem obvious—money, of course—and there is nothing wrong with that. But while no one expects you to have saintly motives, there is so much more to consider than the rich financial rewards of the job. Investment is a very tough business, demanding and competitive, bearing little resemblance to its popular depictions in fiction and cinema. Chances are that you will start off in a job that is more drudgery than high drama. People who enter the business driven only by the visions of wealth and privilege will soon become disillusioned with the real demands of a Wall Street career.

So take time to do a little old-fashioned soul searching before you jump headlong into your career. Even mid-career changers will benefit from this exercise. Whether you want to move from one branch of finance to another, or are coming from an entirely different profession, it helps to parse your goals and weigh them, balance sheet style. The goal of your soul search is to ensure that you enter the business with realistic, attainable goals and with a minimum of illusion. Earning a stratospheric salary does not come easily for most, at least not at the beginning. The learning curve in high finance is steep. It will likely take hard work and exhaustively long hours to master the skills needed to excel in this business. You will need the quant skills of a computer geek, the investigative skills of a muckraking reporter, the persuasiveness of a politician, and the endurance of a long-distance runner. There is also the sacrifice of one's leisure and personal time in the early years of one's career. In many finance fields, the work does not end at 5 o'clock, but continues around the clock, blurring the line between personal and business activities and necessitating the need to be tethered to your smart phone on a 24/7 basis, even on vacations.

For some, of course, the grueling labor is exhilarating. These people thrive on the moment-by-moment intensity and adrenaline-soaked activities of their daily routine. You may be one of these people. If not, you may want to think twice about this type of career choice. This does not mean giving up on an investment career, just choosing the right type of job activity for your personality. Better to think through these issues early on, or you may find yourself writing science fiction for a living like Jules Verne, belatedly seeking a career that better suits your temperament.

This is why recruiters ask candidates to explain themselves and their goals. They are attempting to find out if the candidate has mapped out these larger issues. They want to know if you have the right stuff for an investment career, or if will be someone who will end up dropping out in mid-career. Securities firms want long-term, committed employees, because dropouts are a waste of their corporate resources. Every hire costs the firm money in terms of training and development. Scrutinizing a candidate's goals is just another way of protecting their human resource investment. So when you get asked this question, show the recruiter that you have thought long and hard about the industry and how you will fit into it. Show interest in the firm's goals as well as your own. Ideally, you will paint a picture of yourself as someone who will not just survive, but thrive in the real world of investment.

The MBA

Obtaining an MBA is vital for most careers in the securities industry. It always improves your prospects for hiring and advancement. Your career journey will invariably be easier with it than without it. Think about gliding down a highway in a sports car versus plodding along in a horse and buggy. Some things will just get you to your

Everyone
Knows

What Does a Compliance Officer Do?

The compliance officer is one of the most important executives in an investment firm. The position carries a heavy set of responsibilities, since regulatory lapses or legal entanglements could danger the very existence of the firm. Candidates for this job must have impeccable professional records and be above reproach in every way. Here is a list of common duties carried out by compliance officers:

- Communicates with the SEC, FINRA and other regulatory bodies about filing and other regulatory issues
- Monitors changes in state securities laws and ensures that the firm is in compliance with them
- Ensures that the company meets minimum net capital rules
- Enforces gray list requirements
- Monitors individual and collective employee compliance with applicable laws and internal guidelines
- Responds to customer complaints involving the firm or its employees
- Reviews employees' registrations with the SEC, ensuring that they are properly registered
- Ensures that all employees take any required continuing education classes
- Acts as the company's point person for customer or client complaints about the firm or its employees
- Represents the firm in arbitration proceedings involving customer complaints

destination faster. An MBA gives you the full menu of business and finance skills (accounting, finance, operations, management, marketing, business law), as well as training and practice in things like persuasion and sales skills, leadership training, case management, teamwork, and public speaking. An MBA almost always emphasizes practical skills over theoretical ones. Through tackling hundreds of case studies in the classroom, you will emerge with problem-solving skills for the real world. Most programs will open the door to internship opportunities, part-time consulting, and other real-life work projects. You will make friends with people at business school who may be your colleagues for decades. The opportunity to interact with business professors may also give you valuable contacts, as they can refer you to jobs or to other networking resources. You will emerge from the end of the two-year program with a well rounded education and the skills to successfully tackle most any entry level job in the securities industry. If you are in the middle of your career, going back to school for an MBA may put you on a faster career track, making you eligible for higher compensation and other benefits.

Another consideration is that securities recruiters seem to expect candidates to have the MBA degree and some firms will only consider those with it. In their eyes, the degree shows that you have got the intellectual drive and discipline to succeed in the business. Top-tier firms can afford to be choosy and have the luxury of limiting their short list to MBAs. Since everyone else on their short list will have it, shouldn't you as well? It is about being competitive in an intensely competitive market. Furthermore, once you are in the door and on their payroll, having an MBA will surely put you on a faster career track than those with just the baccalaureate.

The degree is expensive, well into the six-figure range at Ivy League schools, leading some people to wonder whether it is worth it. For most, the cost-benefit analysis works in favor of getting the degree, given the long-term earnings boost it can give you. Yet there is an opportunity cost to getting an MBA that is often overlooked. Try doing the math to determine if it is really worth the time and money in your own case. The analysis can be done by comparing several types of MBA degrees; i.e., from state university to Ivy League to private regional school. The potential for higher earnings must be compared with (1) the tuition and living expenses incurred while in school; (2) the loss of wages incurred by delaying the onset of your career by two years during which you earn no income; and (3) the interest cost of student loans, which can be hefty over the course of years or decades. Just calculating the interest cost alone can be stupefying, leading you to again wonder if an MBA is really worth it. Moreover, contrary to popular perception, the best MBA (in terms of return on your education dollar) may not necessarily be an Ivy

League MBA. But circumstances vary for everyone, so try doing the math to see what options work best for you.

Alternative Ways of Entering the Business

Not everyone can get an MBA right after undergraduate school. Liberal arts majors may not have the preparatory coursework necessary, while others may not be able to immediately afford the steep price tag of an MBA degree. Marital, family, or significant other considerations may also prevent aspiring professionals from getting further education. For whatever reason, some people need to begin their securities career right out of undergraduate college and without the hallowed MBA degree. A mid-career candidate may also not have an MBA, or will hold a non-business graduate degree. The road for these people is paved with difficulty, but it is not an impossible path. A determined individual can work his or her way into the business in other ways. In this context, creativity and resourcefulness are good attributes to have. Here are some of the ways it might be done.

First, consider getting experience at smaller or regional organizations that have more flexible recruiting standards. At the same time, brace yourself for a more modest compensation package from these second-tier firms. While you may not see the hefty sign-on bonuses common to the bulge bracket firms, there will be offsetting advantages. In exchange for lower compensation, you may get the training, experience, or education that you are missing at this point. Many of these firms offer training and leadership development programs for promising candidates. Most companies seem to prefer recent graduates for these programs, although some may consider older candidates in their twenties or thirties. They will sponsor your licensure with the SEC and may even help pay for some of your graduate coursework in accounting, finance, management, and so forth. Some may even help you get your certification. Not every securities firm is amenable to this type of hiring arrangement, but some are. You will probably find securities brokerages more open to hiring and training non-MBA candidates than private equity or wealth management firms, which are buyers' markets in terms of talent acquisition.

These entry-level work/training programs will give you hands-on experience in various parts of the business, and will be an impressive addition to your résumé. A typical path would be to work for this type of employer for at least three years before attempting to move on to the company of your dreams. By the time you are ready to move on, you should have both practical experience and additional education under your belt, preferably, your MBA. However, remember that working on an MBA part-time is a difficult process that may drag out for a long time. While a full-time student can expect to complete an MBA in about two years, a part-time student who is also working full-time will take much longer to complete the degree. It may take four or more years for some people. Moreover, not every MBA program is open to part-timers; some are only available for full-time students. If at the end of three years at the firm you still do not have an MBA in your pocket, do not despair. You can still attempt to move on to your favored employer by using some good sales techniques. Consider using the old-fashioned experience versus education argument, stressing the superiority of your practical experience over purely theoretical knowledge. Many employers will

Fast
Facts

Alternatives to the MBA

More goes on at investment firms than buying stocks or doing deals. These companies may also need specialists in economics, risk management, organizational behavior, taxation, and statistics, to name just a few areas. Here is a list of some graduate degrees that support working in these niches.

- Master of Taxation
- Master of Finance
- Master of Statistics
- Master of Actuarial Science
- Master of Risk Management
- Master of Organizational Behavior
- Master of Economics
- Master of Computer Science
- Master of Mathematics
- Doctor of Philosophy in Economics

be receptive to this pitch, willing to hire an experienced but less-credentialed candidate.

Another possible point of entry to the business is via an internship. This will entail working either for free or for nominal wages in most cases. Consider the idea that you might be better off with an unpaid internship at a top-tier firm than in spending five years at a second tier firm, even at regular salary. Internships often lead to hires, which is precisely why so many firms eagerly accept interns. Not only do they get a lot of grunt work done for free or almost free, they get to scrutinize your work habits in real time and without the normal costs and risks of regular employment. It is common for firms to offer internships to the very candidates they are eying for a permanent position. Smart candidates will recognize this and will use the internship opportunity to show the firm what they can do. At best, the unpaid sojourn can lead to a permanent hire, and at worst it is a great addition to your résumé.

Another alternative career path is to get work experience in an entirely different, but highly relevant area. For example, consider starting your career in government regulation at the national or state level. The relatively modest compensation structures of public sector employment mean lower barriers to entry. Experience in government regulation could be viewed by recruiters as a valuable background for some types of private sector investment careers. Likewise, financial analysts might want to consider starting out in entry-level positions in corporate finance in any type of corporation. These jobs also typically have lower barriers to entry than those in the finance industry. Even better, since most corporations offer educational reimbursement programs, you can use these years to work on an MBA part-time. While the job duties of corporate finance managers differ from those in the securities industry, the experience on the résumé may be good enough for securities employers at a later date, especially if it is accompanied by excellent references and a strong track record of achievements. Another possible pathway is to serve in an entry-level role at a commercial bank, especially helpful if you are able to work in an investment-related job.

When all else fails, fall back on good old-fashioned networking. Use a combination of tried-and-true methods and nontraditional tactics. For example, alumni networks from your college are time-tested sources of contacts, as are your parents' social circles and business acquaintances. Virtual networks may work even faster than real-life ones. Contacts can happen fast through such online outlets as Facebook or Linked In, and do not require that you choke down so many high-calorie hors d'oeuvres.

Find the Firm that is Right for You

One of the most important career decisions you will ever make is choosing a company to work for. It can mean the difference between a fulfilling career and a frustrating one. First, be sure you have your goals and objectives clear to ensure you do not waste your time or a recruiter's time interviewing with a firm that does not suit you (or that you are not suited for). To clarify your goals, walk through the "why investment and why me" exercise discussed at the beginning of this chapter. Once you have a clear picture in mind, develop a short list of firms that meet your criteria. These can come from a variety of sources. The easiest way to identify employers is to have them come to you, through college recruiting venues. For mid-career candidates without an academic affiliation, your best bet is to hang out at job fairs and other public recruiting forums. But do not expect to meet the company of your dreams by these methods alone. The best opportunities may not come knocking on your door, and may require extensive independent research to identify. Some sectors, like hedge funds and private equity, are unlikely to seek out candidates at all, since most receive a steady traffic of stellar résumé s without lifting a finger to recruit. Venture capital firms are also unlikely to actively recruit for the same reasons. Start your research by perusing some of the secondary resources in Chapter 6 (e.g., Hoover's, rankings of business publications, the SEC's registration database) or use the partial list at the end of this chapter to identify some of the major firms in each sector.

Background Checks

Most corporate jobs today require a background check. The financial services industry has even more rigorous standards than most. So be prepared to have your background thoroughly scrutinized. Or better yet, aim to keep your record clean along the way, as the financial services industry has less tolerance than most for blemishes of any kind. Expect at a minimum that the prospective employer will seek to verify your claimed degrees, and that all former employers, including those from internships, will be contacted. Recruiters will also want to ensure that you have a history of compliance with securities industry laws and regulations, that you have not engaged in any workplace theft or violence, and that you are qualified to handle the job for which you are applying. To determine if you have been censured by the SEC or other national or state regulatory body, there will be a check for disciplinary actions and sanctions against you. This may include a search of SEC Administrative Decisions to determine if you have been named in any administrative proceedings or rulings. The FINRA Central Records Depository may also be searched to validate your FINRA registration and other details about your professional background. You can further expect to have your personal credit report scrutinized. Recruiters think (rightly or wrongly) that a negative personal credit history, including late payments or defaulted accounts, indicates that you cannot manage your own money responsibly, and that if you cannot manage your own money, you will not be able to manage theirs. As with most of corporate America, drug tests are becoming more commonplace at financial service firms. Last, you can expect a thorough criminal background check. Any type of criminal history will most likely bar you from working in the securities industry. All in all, brace yourself for a rigorous screening of your background.

Mastering the Art of the Interview

After years of educational training and internships, you have finally landed an interview at the company of your dreams. This in itself should give you confidence, as it means the firm likes what it sees on your résumé. The task now is to bring your résumé to life with a stellar interview performance. Prepare for the interview carefully, as most candidates have just one opportunity to impress. It may help to think of it as a stage performance for which you must meticulously prepare—a one-time opportunity to shape your future. This is not meant to make you overly nervous, just to suggest the importance of attending to many different factors that will shape your image in the eyes of the recruiter.

Start with your personal appearance, as it is the first thing the recruiter will notice when you walk in the door. Your "stage presence" can be as important as the substance of your résumé. As a general rule, you should dress conservatively, even if the company has a casual dress policy for its employees. The financial services industry is not the forum for displaying your iconic personal style in dress or

On the Cutting
Edge

What are Emerging Market Economies?

If the term sounds nebulous, that's because it is. No one has ever come up with an adequate term to describe the countries that make up 80 percent of the world's population—those rapidly growing countries in Africa, Asia, the South Pacific, and Latin America. Among the historic terms used to define this group were *less developed countries, developing economies,* or even *third world economies.* Today, about 40 countries carry the emerging market designation, although the wide variation amongst them points to the continuing problem with the term. For example, an elephantine economy like China is considered to be an emerging market, alongside a small country like Tunisia. What unites all members of this diverse group is their decision to open up their economies to global capital markets, something rarely seen in times past. By any name, emerging markets is one of the hottest investment trends of the early 21st century. Their key characteristic is a potential for high profit, coupled with an equally high potential for risk. Investors searching for superior returns have turned to emerging market equities and bonds, and most firms now have funds devoted exclusively to these securities. As long as these countries need to serve their rapidly rising populations—which will be true for a long time to come— emerging markets will be a major investment opportunity.

hair. Even in the age of Casual Friday, most financial services companies continue to have dress codes for their employees, especially for jobs requiring customer interface. The larger the company, the more likely they will have a strict dress code. Small companies may have more relaxed requirements or no requirements at all, while non-customer-interfacing jobs may even permit blue jeans and sneakers (yes, these companies do exist, even in investment banking).

However, no matter how relaxed a company's dress code may be day-to-day on the job, you should dress formally for the interview. Men who would never wear a suit and tie on the job should nonetheless wear one to an interview. The recruiter will no doubt expect

INTERVIEW

The Competitive Candidate

Karen Ganzlin
Chief Human Resources Officer, TD Ameritrade

What are some of the key challenges facing today's investment professional?

In general, the financial services industry is very competitive. It is fast-paced, in a constant state of change, and requires a lot of energy. It is also one of those sectors where you really need to learn the business. It can be complex, given the broad product spectrum and highly regulated environment. It takes time to progress—to really immerse yourself and become a trusted adviser, or servant, of other people's money.

To be successful, you need to become a student of the industry and embark on lifelong learning. You need to understand the secular trends, including the stock markets, and the business, or how we make money. Building your expertise in these areas will help you build credibility and trust with clients.

What are the most important personal attributes to have if you are interested in a career in investment services?

Understanding the investment business, the offerings, and client service skills are critical. You will not only need to be able to take care of your clients' immediate needs, you will also need to anticipate and address their various life cycle stages and related needs as well so you can create value. Choosing a career in investment services also begs the question, "Why would I trust you with my money?" and for that reason, credibility is just as important. That comes with ample industry and product knowledge, built on a foundation of integrity. You have to be honest beyond reproach. Being a student of the industry is important, and you must be knowledgeable when dealing with people's money and future retirement savings.

What type of training and education do you recommend for a person entering the finance industry today?

Typically, a successful candidate will have a good overall business or economics education and plans to go through a securities licensing program (Series 7 or 63). Even if you do not directly use a securities license, you should still know the material. Understanding the inner workings of the industry is imperative if you plan to move to the next level. Remember, this is a service *and* sales industry. Understanding not only your client value proposition but also how to differentiate it from your competition and communicate those points to your clients and prospects will make you more successful. As such, finely tuned communication skills are a must.

You need to commit to ongoing education. Make a practice of reviewing and analyzing industry trends and what is happening in both the markets and the regulatory environment. Get into the habit of reading the front page of *The Wall Street Journal* and ask yourself, "How could this impact me, my company, or my clients?" This is a fast-paced industry, and change will impact everything you do—from the products you offer to how the stock markets work to how you interact with your clients. What was interesting five years ago may not be today.

What advice would you give to young professionals as to how they can move up the career ladder?

First and foremost you should understand your values (personal and professional), how they align with both the industry and the firm at which you would like to build your career. You should be passionate about living them every day. Alignment is imperative when it comes to driving high employee engagement.

Second, network with others. Meet as many people as possible and be humble about what you do not know. No one expects you to know it all right away. Ask questions and take advantage of outside expertise. Research and know who and what you are.

Third, it is important to perform the job at hand while simultaneously thinking about the next steps in your longer-term career. Sometimes people are too focused on the next job and forget to do today's job. It is a fine balance between being ambitious and staying focused on the task at hand, and you need a great degree of patience as it takes time to become a trusted steward of people's money. Most people are not going to come out of business school and advise and guide clients on their investable assets within six months.

Next, you must be receptive to coaching and feedback. Understand your strengths and weaknesses and accept help where you can to further strengthen your skill set, whether it is a client-facing interaction, a team-building session, or honing your leadership skills.

And finally, I'm a firm believer in the fact that nothing replaces hard work and discretionary effort. Be accountable and accept full responsibility for your actions, goals, and specific deliverables. And sometimes you will be asked to roll up your sleeves and work outside of your assigned duties or area. Nothing is worse than an employee who says, "That's not my job."

(continued on next page)

INTERVIEW

The Competitive Candidate
(continued)

What should aspiring candidates do to make themselves more competitive in the investment job marketplace?
In addition to sales skills and client acumen, leadership skills are very important, especially as you progress into management-level positions. Having solid technical and investment knowledge, along with superior client, management, and leadership skills will set you apart from the competition.

For recent college graduates, a mixture of academic success blended with the right work experience is helpful. We also look at social engagement, community involvement, and other management capabilities that might showcase the potential for leadership.

We are also looking for candidates who can strike a balance between their professional and personal lives. Pursue the things you are passionate about that best align with your values—personally and professionally.

style should blend into the background, drawing no extra attention, and allow the candidate to shine through. While some of this may seem superficial to some (why not judge me by my knowledge of options pricing models?), recruiters, rightly or wrongly, see clues to corporate behavior in a candidate's dress. A black suit on a woman suggests a team player, while pink patent leather shoes suggest an individualist or budding egotist who will not play by the company rules. So allow plenty of time to prepare your personal appearance for the interview, as it can make or break a candidate in many cases. You may even want to do a "dress rehearsal" in front of the mirror a few days before the interview, to see yourself as the recruiter will see you.

Next, prepare for the questions you will get. The interview process offers you the opportunity to prove your merit and convince your prospective employer that you have what it takes to hit the ground running in the competitive world of Wall Street. Following are some of the most common ones.

What are some common mistakes candidates make at interviews or during the hiring process that causes you not to hire them?
Lack of self-awareness can derail you. Do you understand your strengths and weaknesses and, more importantly, can you talk openly about a time when you have been unsuccessful and what you have learned? Someone who can do that, especially at a young age, is quite special.

Doing research on the company before an interview is critical, and that extends beyond reading fact sheets and press releases. Review the vision of the firm, how they make money, and the clients they serve— and consider how you could contribute right away. We want potential candidates to determine if they are a cultural "fit" for the organization they may be joining.

Having realistic career and compensation expectations is very important. Consider whether you are looking for a job or a career. If it is a career, there are tradeoffs. It is a long-term game—a marathon, not a sprint! And, that may mean doing a variety of assignments to round out your skill sets in order to develop your general management skills and meet your longer-term career objectives.

Business is becoming more global, and yet many people are becoming less mobile. Fewer people are willing to move or relocate. You can really put yourself in a competitive advantage if you are willing to relocate for what's often a phenomenal learning opportunity and development assignment—particularly early in your career.

Tell me about yourself.
Believe it or not, many recruiters start out interviews with this vague question. Do not let it overwhelm you, and resist the temptation to give too much detail. The recruiter is not asking for your life story. Do not begin with your lemonade stand in the third grade, even if you are convinced it was the first sign of your entrepreneurial talents. Just provide a brief and succinct summary of your educational background, citing the number of years of experience you have, if any, and any relevant personal facts that might be applicable to the job. For example, if you are applying for an international finance job, a brief reference to having lived abroad might be helpful, along with mentioning the foreign languages you speak. Most importantly, do not ramble and keep all comments relevant to the job for which you are applying.

What are your personal and professional goals?
With this question, the recruiter is looking for evidence that you are committed to the industry and will be a long-term hire. Companies

Professional
Ethics

Case Study: How to Handle Inside Information

Situation: As a stockbroker with a major brokerage firm in Chicago, you know the value of a social networking to bring in clients. You are a fixture on the cocktail party scene and run into people from every industry, including those executives whose tongues are prone to wag under the influence of spirits. You know the rules about insider trading....but, you say to yourself, is there anything wrong with keeping one's ears open? While chatting with a drug company executive over drinks one evening, he tells you *in the strictest of confidence*, that one of his company's key competitors had an application for a certain medical device rejected by the FDA. He does not tell you the competitor's name, but it is obvious to you who the unnamed drug company is—there are only two key players in the market for that product.

Ethical Problem: You are immediately aware of the short selling potential of the information, which could be extraordinarily profitable to anyone who trades on the information. And since, you tell yourself, you did not receive the name of the company, have you really received inside information? Moreover, if you piece together

are looking for candidates who will stay and grow with the company. The question aims to weed out the people who do not know what they want or who have immature goals. People with naïve ideas about getting rich quick, or whose goal is to please their parents will not last long in the securities business. Recruiters hope this question will identify those who are in it for the wrong reasons, and who consequently will end up leaving the firm after a few short years.

Your answer should be crafted to show the recruiter that you have thought through the issues, understand the nature of the business, and have realistic and attainable goals. Also be careful how you express your goals. If you offhandedly mention that you plan to go to law school, the recruiter may perceive you negatively as the executive's information with your own research and analysis—such as using your industry knowledge to deduce who the likely competitor is in this case—is not the information really just the result of good analysis, using the "mosaic theory" of multiple sources of information to form your own conclusion?

Solution: First of all, determine if news about the rejected application is public yet. It may be featured on the front page of tomorrow's *Wall Street Journal.* Second, if you have inadvertently come into possession of inside information, you are professionally obligated to take certain steps. Even if you are not sure the information meets the definition of *material* or *inside*, or if the case might fall in a gray area of legal interpretation, you should still avoid trading in the security. Instead, advise the compliance officer at your firm so he can assess the issue and possibly put the security on a restricted list. Third, encourage the source of the information to take the information public through proper channels, if possible. Fourth, do not disclose the information to others. By and large, investment professionals are ethically and professionally obligated to consider the interests of the investing public. Any information that is not available to the general public or which gives insiders an unfair advantage over the public is inside information, and therefore, prohibited by law.

someone who will be quitting within two years. On the other hand, if you state that you intend to pursue a law degree while working as a junior analyst and hope to one day be a compliance officer, the recruiter will view you as a promising long-term candidate who will bring valuable legal skills to the table.

What academic and educational skills would you bring to this job?
This is a straightforward question that should be answered with the facts of your educational background. Include a summary of your college and university training, concentrating on the amount of financial accounting and computer coursework you have. Internship experience should be noted.

What work experience have you had and what were your major achievements at each of the jobs you have held?

The recruiter will be impressed by a succinct summary of your past work record that mentions the major achievements of each of your past jobs, such as stating the dollar amount you sold per year as a broker, or the dollar volume of deals you did at an investment bank. Internship jobs should be mentioned as well. Employers are looking for a steady record of achievements over time that demonstrates a progressive mastery of skills. This is also the time to capitalize on any specialized training or knowledge you can bring to the table from your last job or last profession. Show the recruiter how your expertise can be harnessed to further the firm's investment goals.

What are the features of your ideal job, in terms of duties, responsibilities, corporate culture and travel responsibilities?

The description you provide the recruiter should match the job for which you are applying. Be sure to do your homework in advance to be sure you understand the firm's corporate culture. If you feel compelled to fabricate your answer slightly—such as not mentioning the fact that you really do not like to travel that much—you may be applying for the wrong job. On the other hand, if you have done your preliminary research, then your description should reassure the recruiter that you are a good match for the job at stake in the application.

Professional Ethics and Standards

People in the securities industry live and breathe money. Every day they are surrounded by the reality or the promise of earning vast sums of money. With so much wealth swirling around them, a very small number of people are lured into devising of ways to beat the system and break the rules. Despite the fact that the overwhelming majority of financial professionals conduct business ethically and legally, recent financial scandals have given the industry a black eye.

With some transgressors, unethical conduct stems from a lack of knowledge or education on basic professional standards. The fault for this may lie with business schools. Even those with MBAs may not have sufficient understanding of their ethical obligations and responsibilities under the law. If there is coursework at all, it has tended to be in the area of compliance and law rather than professional ethics.

Historically, most business schools did not offer classes in ethics, or at least did not require the course to get the degree. The emphasis, instead, has been on the hard business skills needed to succeed. Some of that is changing at some business schools today, as more schools offer classes in this area, but it is certainly not a major trend. One only has to read the newspaper accounts of financial scandals to wonder what business schools have been doing all these years. For these reasons, it is incumbent upon the individual to set his or her ethical compass in the right direction and follow rigorously the guidelines established by regulatory authorities and the professional standards of his practice group.

Making a commitment to adhere to ethical guidelines and industry regulations is possibly the most important step you can take in your early career. Not only is a prison cell a lonely place, being on the receiving end of societal scorn is even lonelier. There is no monetary gain to be made from abusing the rules that is worth the high price that the perpetrator may have to pay. Therefore, take time to review and thoroughly comprehend the concepts of insider trading, material nonpublic information, the Chinese wall, conflicts of interest and gray lists, among other important topics. Your career will depend on it.

Chapter 5

Talk Like a Pro

Nothing impresses recruiters more than a candidate who is fluent in the language of the industry. While it takes years to become fully articulate in finance, there is nothing wrong with using a cheat sheet before a critical interview. The list amasses some of the industry's common terminology, including lexis you may not have learned in MBA school, like the colorful lingo and slang that pepper the conversation of industry insiders. If you would rather not spend your Sunday afternoons rummaging around for your old college textbooks, use this handy guide to refresh your memory before job interviews.

accredited investor Refers to an individual who has a net worth (or joint net worth with spouse) exceeding $1 million, or who has income exceeding $200,000 in each of the last two years (or joint income with spouse exceeding $300,000). Term used in venture and private capital industries.

accrued interest Interest deemed to be earned on a security but not yet paid to the investor.

agency bond A bond issued by a Federal government agency that issues or guarantees bonds for public projects or needs, such as increasing home ownership or providing economic assistance to communities.

agreement among underwriters (AAU) Legal document used principally in negotiated sales by underwriters.

allocation   The amount of securities assigned to an investor, broker, or underwriter in an offering. An allocation can be equal to or less than the amount indicated by the investor during the subscription process depending on market demand for the securities.

alternative investments   An umbrella term for nontraditional investment types, including private equity, venture capital and hedge funds. Alternative investments are generally more risky than traditional investments like stocks or bonds, but the expectation is that they will generate higher returns for investors.

American depositary receipt (ADR)   A dollar-denominated certificate which denotes a specified number of shares in a foreign stock that is traded on a U.S. exchange.

American Stock Exchange (AMEX)   The second largest stock exchange in the United States, located in the financial district of New York City. It was once known as the Curb Exchange, a reference to the fact that it originally conducted trades on the street curbs of lower Manhattan.

amortization   Accounting for expenses as applicable rather than when paid, and which may include such practices as depreciation, write-off, and depletion.

angel financing   Private capital raised for a new company from independently wealthy investors. This capital is generally used as seed financing or start-up capital.

angel investor   A person who provides backing to very early stage businesses or new ventures. Angel investors are typically very wealthy and must also be financially strong enough to make risky investments, which new ventures typically are.

arbitrage   In the municipal bond market, the difference in interest earned on funds borrowed at a lower tax-exempt rate and interest on funds invested at a higher-yielding taxable rate.

archangel   A person hired by a syndicate of angel investors to carry out due diligence on investment opportunities. Archangels typically have no financial commitment to the syndicate or investment.

ask price (or offer price)   The price at which a security is offered for sale.

ask yield   The return investors would receive on a U.S. Treasury security if they paid the ask price.

asset allocation   An investment strategy in which an investor divides assets among different several categories of investments to reduce risk in an investment portfolio while maximizing return.

asset-backed securities (ABS)   Asset-backed securities, called ABS, are bonds or notes backed by financial assets other than residential or commercial mortgages—an investor is purchasing an interest in pools of financial assets. The ABS securities are for institutional investors and are not suitable for individual investors.

asset class   A category or type of investment that has similar characteristics and behaves similarly when subject to particular market forces. The major asset classes are stocks, bonds and cash. Real estate, precious metals and commodities can also be viewed as asset classes.

assets   Anything of tangible or intangible of economic value owned by a business or individual.

auction   Sealed-bid public sale of Treasury securities.

auction rate bonds   Floating-rate tax-exempt bonds where the rate is periodically reset by a Dutch auction.

auction market   The system of trading securities in which buyers enter bids and sellers enter offers simultaneously. The buyers and sellers are represented by brokers on the exchange. An order is executed when matching bids and offers are paired together.

authorizing resolution   An issuer document that states the legal basis for debt issuance, and states the general terms of the financing.

averages   A way of measuring the trend of securities prices over a time period. One of the best known averages is the Dow Jones Industrial Average, which tracks 30 industrial stocks listed on the New York Stock Exchange.

average annual yield   The average yearly income on an investment expressed in percentage terms. To calculate average annual yield, add all the income from an investment and divide the total by the number of years in which the money will be invested.

basis point   One one-hundredth (.01) of a percentage point. For example, six percent would be equal to 600 basis points.

basis price   The price of a security expressed in yield, or percentage of return on the investment.

bear   An investor who trades on the belief that the market is going to decline.

Fast Facts

The Bulge Bracket

In common parlance, "bulge bracket" refers to a subset of investment banks that are widely considered to be the largest and most powerful in the world. Global in scope, these firms have clients across the world, including blue chip and large multinational corporations, institutions and governments. Bulge bracket firms are frequently the innovators of new financial products, like the credit default swap or the mortgage-backed security. The list changes from time to time, most recently since the 2008 subprime mortgage crisis, when several key players (like Bear Stearns and Lehman Brothers) lost their position on the enviable list.

bearer bond   A physical bond that does not identify the owner and is assumed to be owned by the person holding it. The only bearer bonds still in existence in the secondary market were issued prior to 1982.

benchmark   A bond whose terms are used for comparison with other bonds of similar maturity. The global financial market typically looks to U.S Treasury securities as benchmarks.

bid   Price at which a buyer is willing to purchase a security.

bid-ask spread   The difference between the highest price a buyer is willing to pay for an asset (i.e., stock) and the lowest price for which a seller is willing to sell it.

Big Board   A nickname for the New York Stock Exchange.

bill   A short-term obligation of the U.S. Treasury that has a maturity of not more than one year

blended yield to maturity   The combination and average of two points on the yield curve to find a yield at the midpoint.

blue chip   The stock of a well-established and financially healthy company, generally expected to have stable and reliable growth over the long-term.

blue-sky memorandum   A memorandum that specifies the way an issue will be treated under state securities laws of the fifty states, Puerto Rico, and District of Columbia.

bond   The written document of a debt. It bears the stated interest rate and maturity date.

bond anticipation note (BAN)   A note issued in anticipation of later issuance of bonds, usually payable from the proceeds of the sale of the bonds.

bond fund   An investment vehicle which invests in a portfolio of bonds which is professionally managed. Among the types of bond funds are open-ended mutual funds, closed-end mutual funds, and exchange traded funds.

bond insurers and reinsurers   Insurance firms serving the fixed-income market that guarantee the timely payment of principal and interest on bonds they insure in exchange for a fee.

bond purchase agreement (BPA)   The purchase contract between the issuer and the underwriter setting forth the terms of the sale, including the price of the bonds, the interest rate of the bonds, and the conditions to closing.

bond resolution   The issuer's legal document, detailing the bond's security features, covenants, events of default, and legal features.

book entry   An electronic method of recording ownership of securities, which eliminates the need for physical certificates.

broker   A firm or person who acts as an intermediary by buying and selling securities to dealers on an agency basis rather than for its own account.

brokers' loans   Money borrowed by securities brokers, generally from banks. Funds are used to purchase stocks, to underwrite new issues of corporate and municipal securities, to finance the securities firm's own portfolio, or to purchase securities for customers who prefer to buy them with credit.

bubble   A cyclical expansion of the economy, followed by sharp contraction; also denotes a strong rise in a stock's price that is unjustified by its underlying value, followed by a selloff.

Build America Bonds (BABs)   Taxable municipal bonds authorized under the American Recovery and Reinvestment Act of 2009; unlike most municipal bonds, BABs are subject to taxation.

bull   An investor who trades on the belief that the market is going to decline.

bullet bond   A bond that pays regular interest, but that does not repay principal until maturity.

bull market   An advancing market, or one in which the trend line is headed up.

bull position   A stock trade done in the hope that the price will rise. It is the opposite of a bear position, which is initiated in the hope that the stock's price will fall.

buy side   The part of a firm's securities business in which institutional orders originate.

call   An action taken to pay the principal amount prior to the stated maturity date, in accordance with the provisions for calls outlined in the original agreement.

call date   The date at which some bonds are redeemable by the issuer prior to the maturity date.

call premium   The dollar amount paid to the investor by the issuer for exercising a call provision.

call price   The specified price at which a bond will be redeemed prior to maturity, typically either at a premium or at par.

callable bonds   Bonds redeemable by the issuer prior to the maturity date, at a specified price.

cap   The maximum interest rate that can be paid on a floating-rate security.

capital appreciation   A rise in the value of an asset based on a rise in market price. It is one source of return on investment, the others being dividends or interest income.

capital gain   The gain made by the investor from selling a stock, bond or mutual fund at a higher price than the purchase price, net of sales costs and taxes.

capital markets   The electronic and physical markets in which financial instruments are sold to investors.

capital under management   The amount of capital available to a management team for investing in new ventures.

captive fund   A venture capital firm owned by a larger financial institution, such as a bank.

carry   The cost of borrowing funds to finance an underwriting or trading position.

cash dividend   Periodic money paid to stockholders, normally out of the company's current or accumulated earnings.

catch-up   A term used in private equity partnership agreements. Once the general partner provides its limited partners with their preferred return, it enters a "catch-up" period in which it receives the profits until such time as the agreed upon profit-split, is reached.

certificate   The physical piece of paper that shows proof of stock ownership in a corporation. To discourage fraud or forgery, it is printed on watermarked or finely engraved paper.

CFTC   Acronym for the U.S. Commodity Futures Trading Commissions.

Chinese wall   A barrier against information flows between different divisions or operating groups within securities firms. A common example is the barrier against information sharing between corporate finance and equity research and trading operations.

clean price   Price of a bond excluding accrued interest. Bond prices are usually quoted "clean."

closed-end mutual fund   A fund created with a fixed number of shares, which are traded as a security on a stock exchange.

closing bell   The traditional use of a bell ring to signify the end of a day's trading session. Today's closing bell is at 4 P.M. EST at the New York Stock Exchange.

closing price   The price of a bond or stock at the very end of the market trading day.

collar   Upper and lower limits of the interest rate on a floating-rate security.

collateralized debt obligation (CDO)   A type of asset-backed security (ABS), CDOs are backed by fixed income assets such as bonds, receivables on loans—usually nonmortgage—or other debt that have different levels of risk.

collateralized mortgage obligation (CMO)   A multiclass bond backed by a pool of mortgage pass-through securities or mortgage loans.

commercial paper   Short-term, unsecured bond notes issued by a corporation or a bank to meet immediate short term needs for cash. It is usually issued by companies with high credit ratings and sold at a discount from face value.

commission   The fee paid to a dealer when the dealer acts as agent in a transaction.

committed capital   The total dollar amount of capital pledged to a private equity fund.

common stock   A share representing participation in the ownership of a company, generally with the right to vote on issues affecting stockholder interests.

competitive underwriting or sale   A sale of municipal securities by an issuer in which underwriters submit sealed bids to purchase the securities.

composite Index   A grouping of equities, indexes or other elements which provide a measurement of overall market, industry, or sector performance over a period of time.

compound interest   Interest that is calculated on the original principal and interest paid.

compounding   The process by which earnings are added to investment principal to form a larger amount on which to earn additional interest or return over time.

consolidated tape   The combined ticker tape transactions in NYSE securities that take place on the NYSE and any of the participating regional stock exchanges.

convertible bond   A corporate bond that can be exchanged for a specific number of shares of the company's stock.

convertible preferred stock   A type of preferred stock that includes an option to convert the shares into common shares after a specified date.

convexity   A measure of the change in a security's duration with respect to changes in interest rates. The more convex a security is, the more its duration will change with interest rate changes.

conversion ratio   The number of shares of stock into which a convertible security may be converted. The conversion ratio equals the par value of the convertible security divided by the conversion price.

convertible security   A bond, debenture or preferred stock that is exchangeable for another type of security (usually common stock) at a predetermined price.

Everyone Knows

Some Things Never Change

For those interested in private equity jobs, the old rules still apply. Old-fashioned connections count more than anything else in landing a good job. That is because the industry does not advertise jobs very often, so you cannot rely on published job sites to find the entry-level openings. Instead, rely on traditional networking techniques or work in a field that puts you in contact with the key players. For example, working as a management consultant on private equity issues will get your foot in the door and give you the best shot at showing off your skills.

corporate bond   Bonds issued by corporations. Corporations use the funds they raise from selling bonds for a variety of purposes, from building facilities to purchasing equipment to expanding their business.

coupon   A feature of a bond that denotes the amount of interest due and the date payment is to be made. Zero-coupon bonds are those where the coupon is blank.

coupon payment   The actual dollar amount of interest paid to an investor. The amount is calculated by multiplying the interest of the bond by its face value.

coupon rate   The interest rate on a bond, shown as a percentage of the bond's face value, usually expressed on a semi-annual basis.

covenant   In financing documents, the issuer's promise to do or not to do certain practices and actions.

cover bid   The second-highest bidder in a competitive sale.

covered bond   Debt securities backed by a guarantee from the issuing entity and secured by a dynamic pool of assets on that entity's balance sheet. The issuer is typically a regulated financial institution.

credit enhancement   The use of the credit of a stronger entity to strengthen the credit of a weaker entity in bond or note financing.

credit rating agency   A company that analyzes the credit worthiness of a company or security, and designates that credit quality by means of a credit rating.

credit risk   The risk for bond investors that the issuer will default on its obligation (default risk) or that the bond value will decline and/or that the bond price performance will compare unfavorably to other bonds against which the investment is compared.

currency risk   Occurs when an investor buys a government bond not denominated in his or her home currency. In these cases, the investor faces the risk that changes in the currency exchange rate between the home country and the foreign country will cause a decline in the value of the bond.

current yield   The ratio of the interest rate payable on a bond to the actual market price of the bond, stated as a percentage.

CUSIP   The Committee on Uniform Security Identification Procedures was established by the American Bankers Association to develop a uniform method of identifying securities.

cyclical stock   A stock that performs in accordance with economic cycles, rising quickly when overall economic growth is strong and falling swiftly when overall economic growth declines.

dated date   The date of a bond issue on which the bond begins to accrue interest.

day order   An order to buy or sell that is good for only one trading day and which will expire if not executed by close of the same day.

dealer   A securities firm that engages in the underwriting, trading and sale of various types of securities.

debenture   An unsecured debt obligation, issued against the general credit of a corporation, rather than against a specific asset.

debt financing   Type of financing derived from selling bonds, bills, or notes to investors, who receive interest in return.

debt limit   Statutory limit on the principal amount of debt that an issuer may incur (or that it may have outstanding at any one time).

deep discount   A discount greater than traditional market discounts of 3 percent.

default   The failure by an issuer to pay principal or interest when due or to comply with certain covenants in the indenture.

default risk   The possibility that a bond issuer will fail to pay principal or interest when it is due.

deficiency letter   An SEC letter sent to a new issuer regarding omissions of material fact in its registration statement.

delisting   The removal of a listed security from the stock exchange. The delisting can be either voluntary or involuntary. Usually, delisting occurs when the stock is not meeting the listing requirements of the exchange.

denomination   The face amount of a bond or note that the issuer promises to pay on the maturity date.

derivative   A financial product that derives its value from an underlying security.

desk trader   A securities trader restricted to executing trades for his or her firm's clients and who does not trade with the firm's own accounts.

direct financing   Direct financing is a financing without the use of underwriting. Direct financing is often done by investment bankers.

dirty price   Price of a bond including accrued interest.

discos   Agency bond no-coupon discount notes ("discos") issued by federal agencies to meet short-term financing needs that are issued at a discount to par value.

discount   The amount by which the par value of a security exceeds its purchase price.

discount bond   A bond sold at less than par value.

discount broker   An agent that executes orders between securities buyers and sellers at low commission rates or even for a flat fee per trade. As a tradeoff for the lower commissions, they provide fewer services to clients than standard brokers.

discount note   Short-term obligations issued at a discount from face value, with maturities ranging from one to 360 days.

discount rate   The key interest rates central banks charge on overnight loans to commercial and member banks. In the United States, the term means the interest rate used by the Federal Reserve on loans to its member banks.

discretionary account   An account in which the customer gives the broker the authority to trade on his behalf, including making decisions on the choice, amount, price, and timing of trades.

diversification   A strategy by which an investor distributes investments among different asset classes or through other diversification techniques. The strategy protects the portfolio value in the event of changes in market conditions or other risks.

dividend per share (DPS)   The total dividends paid out over a year divided by the number of ordinary shares outstanding.

dollar bond   A bond that is quoted and traded in dollar prices rather than in terms of yield.

double and triple tax-exemption   Securities that are exempt from state and local taxes are said to have double tax-exemption; if they are also exempt from federal income taxes, they have triple tax-exemption.

double-barreled bond   A bond is referred to as double-barreled if it is secured by the pledge of two or more payment sources.

Dow Jones Industrial Average (DJIA)   One of the best-known and most widely quoted of the stock market indexes. DJIA is a price-weighted average of 30 major stocks traded on the New York Stock Exchange and the Nasdaq. Other stock indexes include the Dow Jones Transportation Average (DJTA), the Dow Jones Wilshire Large-Cap Index (composite of top 750 companies ranked by market cap), and the Dow Jones Utility Average—DJUA (composite of 15 major utilities).

downgrade risk   The possibility that a bond's rating will be lowered due to the worsening of an issuer's financial condition.

drive-by deal   Jargon used to designate venture capital deal entered into with the intent to make a quick exit from the venture (i.e., a quick sell-off).

dual-currency bonds   Bonds—usually foreign bonds—in which principal payments are in one currency and coupon payments are in another currency.

due diligence   The research undertaken by potential investors for the purpose of analyzing and assessing the value and potential of an investment opportunity.

Dutch auction   In the context of debt securities, a type of auction wherein a competitive bidding process establishes the interest rate of the security. It is also used in reference to U.S. Treasury auctions.

early stage   The period of time in which a new company has completed its initial funding or seed stage and has a management team in place. Other benchmarks include having a viable product that has completed its initial testing phase, as well as showing some revenues, though no positive earnings.

economic indicator   A statistical measure of current conditions in an economy. Economic indicators together provide a picture of the overall health of an economy

economic risk   The vulnerability of a security or investment to downturns in the economy.

EDGAR Public Dissemination Service (PDS)   Available on the SEC Web site (http://www.sec.gov), EDGAR PDS is an online service that allows anyone to download EDGAR documents (corporate filings, registration statements) submitted by public companies to the SEC.

elevator pitch   An extremely concise presentation to venture capitalists of an entrepreneur's core concept, including business model, marketing strategy, and competition. The term refers to the fact that the length of the presentation should be brief, no longer than the duration of an elevator ride.

emerging market bonds   Government and corporate bonds issued within an emerging market country—those countries formerly referred to as developing countries, or "third-world nations."

EMMA   The acronym for the Municipal Securities Rulemaking Board's, Electronic Municipal Market Access, an electronic repository for municipal issuers' disclosure documents. It offers real-time access to bond and note price information.

equity fund   A mutual fund that invests primarily in stocks. It is also known a stock fund.

equity kicker   Option included in a contract wherein private equity investors have the option to purchase shares at a discount. The concept is typically associated with mezzanine financings where a small number of shares or warrants is added to what is primarily a debt financing.

ethical investing   An investment strategy that uses a set of ethical guidelines to choose stocks and other investments. Some ethical investors eliminate entire industries (tobacco, firearms, alcohol), while others review companies on a case-by-case basis for ethical practices. Also known as socially responsible investing.

Eurobond   Bonds denominated in a currency other than that of the European country in which they are issued.

exchangeable bond   A bond with the option to exchange it for shares in a company other than the issuer company.

exchange-traded fund   A passively managed fund that tracks an index, a commodity or basket of assets and which is traded like a stock on an exchange.

ex-dividend   A shortcut way of stating that a stock has no dividend.

exercise price   The price at which an option or warrant can be exercised.

exiting climates   The market, industry or economic conditions that influence the viability and attractiveness of various exit strategies.

exit strategy   A private fund's plan for liquidating its holdings while achieving the maximum possible return. These strategies will depend on various factors, such as future market conditions and industry trends. Exit strategies can include selling the company's shares after an IPO or selling the company.

expected maturity date   The date on which principal is projected to be paid to investors. It is based on assumptions about collateral performance.

extraordinary redemption   A redemption that is different from optional redemption or mandatory redemption because it is triggered by an unusual circumstance such as a natural disaster affecting the underlying asset.

face or par value   The principal amount of a security as it appears on the face of the instrument, and as distinct from market value.

fallen angel   A formerly investment-grade corporate bond which has been downgraded by a credit rating agency due to the deterioration of the issuer's financial status.

52-week high/low   The highest and lowest stock price during the past 52 weeks.

financial adviser   A consultant who provides clients with advice on investing in securities of all types, as well as providing strategic counsel on portfolio issues.

Financial Industry Regulatory Authority (FINRA)   The largest nongovernmental regulator for securities firms doing business in the United States. FINRA was created in 2007 by the merger of the NASD and the regulatory and enforcement arms of the NYSE.

financial and operations principal   A municipal securities employee who is required to prepare and file financial reports to the SEC and other regulatory bodies, as established by the MSRB.

fixed-rate bond   A long-term bond with a set interest rate to maturity.

floating-rate bond   A bond whose interest rate is adjusted periodically according to a predetermined formula or interest rate.

floating stock   Shares of a company freely available for purchase on the secondary market.

floor   The massive trading area of the NYSE where all securities trading is done, often compared to the size of a football field.

floor broker   A member who executes orders on the floor of a stock exchange.

Form 10-K   The annual report which public companies must file with the SEC, providing a detailed and comprehensive picture of the company's financial operations. The report must be filed within 90 days after the end of the company's fiscal year.

Form 10-KSB   The annual report filed by small business issuers. It provides a comprehensive overview of the company's business, although its requirements call for slightly less detailed information than required by Form 10-K. The report must be filed within 90 days after the end of the company's fiscal year.

full disclosure   The SEC requirement that publicly traded companies release all material facts about their ongoing business operations for the purpose of informing investors interested in purchasing its stocks or other securities. The objective of full disclosure is to give confidence to investors and make the marketplace efficient and orderly.

fundamentals research   Analysis of industries and companies based on such "fundamental" factors as sales, assets, earnings, products, marketing, and management.

fund of funds   A mutual fund which invests in other mutual funds for the purpose of achieving optimal diversification.

futures   A contract between two parties who agree to buy or sell a specified amount of an underlying financial instrument at a specific price on a specific day in the future. The price is agreed to at the time of the contract. Among the common types are interest rate futures, stock index futures, and currency futures.

future value   The value of an asset at a specified date in the future, calculated using a specified rate of return.

general obligation bond (GO)   A municipal bond secured by the pledge of the issuer's full faith, credit, and taxing power.

glamour stock   The same as growth stock—shares whose earnings are expected to grow at an above-average rate relative to the market; these stocks typically do not pay dividends, but are purchased for their capital appreciation potential.

going private   The process of making a publicly traded company a private entity. Often involves the company's management decision to buy out the public shares, or when an individual or institution offers to buy the company's stock from existing shareholders.

going public   Generally known as an initial public offering, it is the process of selling formerly private shares on a public exchange for the first time.

greenmail   Often seen in hostile takeovers, greenmail is a term used to describe a situation where a large block of stock is held by a hostile corporate shareholder, thereby forcing the target of the takeover to pay a substantial premium to repurchase the stock, or face imminent takeover.

hedge   An investment made with the intention of minimizing the impact of adverse price movements in an asset or liability, offsetting potential losses.

high-yield bond (or junk bond)   Bonds rated Ba (by Moody's) or BB (by Standard and Poor's) or below, which are considered to be lower credit ratings that indicate a higher risk of default, but which also are issued at a higher yield than higher rated bonds.

illiquid   A situation in which there is insufficient cash flow to meet financial debts or obligations.

incubator   An organization formed to help entrepreneurs develop and implement new business ideas; typically, the incubator will offer advice, management expertise, resources, and intellectual capital.

indenture   Legal document which details security features, covenants, events of default and other key features of the bond issuer's legal and financial status.

industrial revenue bond   A security issued by a state, agency or other political authority for certain official purposes, and which are backed by the credit of a private enterprise.

inflation   The rate of increase in the price of goods and service, usually measured on an annualized basis.

inflation-indexed securities   Securities with its principal adjusted to reflect the effects of inflation with the aim of protecting the holder from future adverse effects of inflation.

initial delivery   The delivery of a new security by the issuer to the original purchaser, upon payment of the purchase price.

institutional investors   Large organizational entities with significant amounts of money to invest and high-level investment expertise; common examples are unit trusts, pension funds, and insurance companies.

interest   Compensation paid to borrow money, generally expressed as an annual percentage rate.

Intermarket Trading System (ITS)   An electronic communications system that interconnects the trading floors of seven competing exchanges and FINRA, the purpose of which is encourage price competition among the participating exchanges.

investment bank   A financial intermediary that performs underwriting services, acts as an intermediary between an issuer of securities and investors, facilitates mergers and corporate reorganizations, and acts as a broker for institutional clients.

investment-grade bond (or high grade bond)   Bonds rated Baa (by Moody's) or BBB (by Standard and Poor's) or better, whose higher credit ratings indicate a lower risk of default.

IO (interest-only) security   A security or tranche that pays only interest and not principal.

ISIN   The numbering code system set up by the International Organization for Standardization and used by internationally traded securities to identify and number each issue of securities.

issuer   The entity obligated to pay principal and interest on a bond it issues.

junior security A security with a claim on a corporation's assets and income that is subordinate or secondary to that of a senior security. For example, common stock is junior to preferred stock.

laddering A technique for reducing the impact of interest-rate risk by structuring a portfolio with different bond issues that mature at different dates.

level debt service A debt service schedule where total annual principal plus interest is approximately the same throughout the life of the bond.

level principal A debt service schedule where total annual principal plus interest declines throughout the life of the bond.

leverage The use of borrowed money to increase investing power.

leveraged buy-out (LBO) The acquisition of a business using mostly debt and a small amount of equity. The debt is secured by the assets of the business. The company being acquired generally expects its future cash flows to cover loan payments.

Liberty bonds A special type of tax-exempt bond created to boost construction or renovation of residential property within the Liberty Zone in Lower Manhattan, New York, and commercial property within New York City primarily in the Liberty Zone following the September 11, 2001, terrorist attacks.

London Interbank Offered Rate (LIBOR) The interest rate banks charge each other for short-term Eurodollar loans, and frequently used as the base for resetting rates on floating-rate securities.

limited partnership An entity formed under state law that allows a group of investors to become limited partners of a partnership unit, owning an economic interest in the entity's assets, but sharing in its liabilities only to the extent of their initial investment.

limited-liability company A company incorporated under state laws that is structured as a "pass-through" entity and treated like a partnership for tax purposes.

liquidation value The amount a securities holder may receive in case of a liquidation of the issuer.

liquidity A measure of the relative ease and speed with which a security can be purchased or sold in the secondary market.

long-term debt Debt which matures in more than one year.

margin The amount paid by the customer when using a broker's credit to buy or sell a security. The percentage amount of the margin is regulated by the Federal Reserve.

margin call   The requirement that a customer put up money or securities as collateral with his broker when a stock purchase is made on margin.

market price   For securities traded through an exchange, the last reported price at which a security was sold.

maturity date   The date when the principal amount of a security is due to be repaid.

maturity schedule   The listing, by dates and amounts, of principal maturities of an issue.

monetary default   Failure to pay principal or interest promptly when due.

money market fund   A type of mutual fund that is invested in money market securities, such as treasury bills, certificates of deposit, and commercial paper.

mortgage pass-through security   A debt instrument representing a direct interest in a pool of mortgage loans. The pass-through issuer collects payments on the loans and "passes through" the principal and interest to the security holders.

mortgage-backed bonds (MBS)   Bonds or notes backed by mortgages on residential or commercial properties, generally suited only for institutional investors.

municipal bond   A bond issued by a state or local governmental unit.

Municipal Securities Rulemaking Board (MSRB)   A self-regulatory organization with primary rulemaking authority over dealers, dealer banks, and brokers in municipal securities; it also distributes market information and operates the Electronic Municipal Market Access (EMMA) Web site for the purpose of promoting transparency in the municipal bond market.

NASDAQ   The acronym for the National Association of Securities Dealers Automated Quotation, it is an automated information network providing price quotes for over-the-counter securities.

new-issue market   Market for new issues of bonds and notes

New York Futures Exchange (NYFE)   A subsidiary of the New York Stock Exchange involved in the trading of futures and related products.

New York Stock Exchange (NYSE)   The largest organized securities market in the United States, made up of about 1,366 individual members and governed by a board of directors. Founded in 1792, it is now owned by the NASD.

nominal value The face value of a bond (as opposed to the amount an individual investor might have paid for the bond).

noncallable bond A bond that cannot be called for redemption by the issuer before its specified maturity date.

noninvestment grade Bonds not considered suitable for preservation of capital; ordinarily, those rated Baa3 or below by Moody's or BBB- or below by Standard and Poor's.

odd lot Refers either to blocks of bonds of $100,000 or less, or to an amount of stock less than the standard 100-share unit.

offer The price at which a seller offers to sell a security.

offering document The disclosure document prepared by a bond or note issuer that gives in detail security and financial information about the issuer and instrument.

offering price The price at which members of an underwriting syndicate for a new issue will offer securities to investors.

order period Specific length of time when orders for new issues are placed by investors.

original face The face value or original principal amount of a security on its issue date.

over-the-counter market (OTC) An electronic securities market conducted by dealers throughout the country through negotiation of price rather than through the use of an auction system as represented by a stock exchange.

paper profit (loss) An unrealized profit or loss on a security still held. Actual profits and losses are realized when the security is sold.

principal and interest (PandI) The term used to refer to regularly scheduled payments or prepayments of principal and of interest on mortgage securities.

par Price equal to the face amount of a security; 100 percent.

participation Principal amount of bonds to be underwritten by each syndicate member.

paying agent The entity, usually a bank or the treasurer of the issuer that pays the principal and interest of a bond.

payment date The date that principal and interest payments are paid to the owner of a security.

penny stocks Stocks priced very low, often at less than $1.00 per share. They are generally viewed as low-grade, risky and speculative equity investments.

performance An investment's return (usually total return), compared to a benchmark or standard of measurement.

perpetual floating-rate note   A floating-rate note with no stated maturity date.

portfolio   A group of securities held by individuals or institutions, which typically includes a mix of different types of assets.

preferred stock   An equity security that is junior to the issuing entity's debt obligations but senior to common stock in the payment of dividends and liquidation of assets. Preferred stock usually has no voting rights and frequently has a redemption provision.

premium   The amount by which the price of a security exceeds its principal amount.

premium or discount price   When the dollar price of a bond is above its face value, it is said to be selling at a premium. (When the dollar price is below face value, it is said to be selling at a discount.)

present value   The current value of a future payment or stream of payments, given a specified interest rate; also referred to as a discount rate.

price-to-earnings ratio   The price of a share of stock divided by earnings per share for a 12-month period. It is a common way to gauge the price performance of the stock.

primary market   The market for new issues.

principal   The face amount of a bond, exclusive of accrued interest and payable at maturity.

Best Practice

The Slow Track

Impatience is a common trait among young professionals. But while you may be eager to move quickly up the career ladder, it is possible to move too fast, causing you to be viewed as "pushy" by your colleagues. Entry-level hires in brokerage or investment banking firms are expected to "pay their dues," regardless of how qualified they may be. Two years as an analyst followed by a few more years as an associate is common. So take a deep breath, slow down, and build your career deliberately and gradually. It will pay bigger dividends down the road.

private placement The negotiated offering of new securities directly to investors, without a public underwriting.

pro rata Proportional distribution to all holders of the same class, based on ownership.

prospectus Selling documents provided to investors who are considering investing in securities registered with the SEC. The prospectus details the investment's objectives, the nature of the investment, past performance, information on the investment company or managers, and other material information.

proxy The written authorization of a shareholder to another person to represent him or her at a shareholders' meeting, and which may include voting rights.

put bond A bond that gives the holder the right to require the issuer to purchase the bonds at a price, usually at par, at some date prior to the final maturity date.

put option Allows the holder of a bond to "put," or present, the bond to an issuer and demand payment at a stated time before the final stated maturity of the bond.

ratings Designations used by credit rating agencies to rate or grade the credit quality of instrument.

recession A downturn in overall U.S. economic activity, which is defined as two or more quarters of decline in output, as measured by gross national product or gross domestic product.

redemption The paying off or buying back of a bond by the issuer; also, repurchase of investment trust units by the trustee, at the bid price.

redemption date The date on which the bond's term ends and the principal amount of a security is payable along with any final interest payment.

redemption yield Annual percentage return received by investor if the bond is held to maturity, a calculation often used to compare bonds. Also called yield to maturity.

red herring A registration statement that has been filed, but not approved, by the SEC.

registered bond A bond whose owner is registered with the issuer or its agent.

registered owner The name in which a security is registered, as stated on the certificate or on the books of the paying agent.

registration The requirement that a company register with the SEC pursuant to the rules of the Securities Act of 1933.

Registration must be made and approved before the initial public offering is made. The registration documents must disclose information about the company's operations, management and other business and investment issues.

Regulation C   SEC rule outlining registration and filing requirements under terms of the Securities Act of 1933 (17 CFR 230.401—230.498).

Regulation D   SEC rule governing the offer and sale of securities without registration under the Securities Act of 1933 (17 CFR 230.501—230.508).

Regulation S   SEC rule governing the offer and sale of securities made outside the United States without registration under the Securities Act of 1933(17 CFR 230.901—230.905).

Regulation T   A Federal Reserve regulation governing the amount of credit that may be advanced by brokers and dealers to customers for the purchase of securities.

Regulation U   A Federal Reserve regulation which defines the amount of credit that can be advanced by banks to customers for the purchase of stocks.

reinvestment risk   The risk that interest income or principal repayments will have to be reinvested at lower rates in a declining interest rate environment.

repurchase agreements (repos)   An agreement between a seller and a buyer, typically of U.S. government securities, whereby the seller "sells" the securities to the buyer, while simultaneously agreeing to repurchase the securities at a stipulated price on some future date.

retail investors   Individual investors who invest relatively small amounts of money in the markets, as compared to institutional investors.

revenue bond   A municipal bond payable from income derived from tolls, charges, or rents paid by users of the facility that has been constructed with the proceeds of the bond issue.

rights offering   When issued to shareholders, allows them to purchase additional shares, usually at a discount to market price. Rights are usually often sellable on the open market.

risk   A measure of the degree of uncertainty or potential for financial loss inherent in an investment. Among the several types of risk are credit risk (the risk that the issuer of the bonds will be unable to make debt service payments due to

Problem
Solving

Case Study: Signing Bonus vs. Salary

Situation: Just as your job search enters its third month, you are thrilled to get a job offer from a top mutual fund firm in southern California. Tuckered out from résumé writing, you are eager to roll up your sleeves, get working on your tan, and start the new job as soon as possible. But since it is your first job out of college, you are a little green on the mechanics of hiring, especially negotiating the best compensation package. In the back of your mind is the fact that your long-term goal is to start your own firm, which may limit your time with this firm to five years.

Problems: How much importance should you place on the size of the signing bonus? Who gets offered a bonus and why? What does it mean if you do not get offered a bonus? In what cases should you consider an offer with no bonus at all?

Solution: Experienced investment pros, especially those with out-standing performance records, will easily command a bonus. Companies use the bonus to sweeten the deal, i.e., to make their offer more attractive than the competitor's next door. The story is different for recent graduates getting hired for their first time. Although today's graduate has been conditioned to expect bonuses, the truth is that eye-popping compensation packages—the upper five-figure sign-ons—are usually reserved for Ivy League graduates or top-of-the-class MBAs from prominent universities. Those without an MBA or with blemishes on their record (you know who you are) may be offered no bonus at all. But unless your record has a major defect, you should confidently approach any negotiation expecting to receive a major portion of your compensation in the form of a bonus. The rule of thumb for experienced and mid-career professionals is to negotiate a bonus of 7 to 10 percent of their annual base salary. For those "high-value targets" (you too know who you are), the sky is the limit and can be as much as the market for your talents will bear.

unanticipated changes, such as a corporate restructuring, a regulatory change or an accident, in their environment); market risk (potential price fluctuations in a security due to changes in the general level of interest rates); and underwriting risk (the risk

When analyzing a compensation package, try putting yourself in the employer's shoes. Consider what the employer hopes to accomplish with the bonus. Among the reasons are:

1. To encourage loyalty and longevity.
Many bonuses come with strings attached: they are paid out only after the hiree has completed a set period of employment—say, eight years. Others require that you pay the firm back if you leave early. So it is vital that you review the fine print of the employment contract. Be sure you understand *when* and *under what conditions* you will receive the bonus. Despite the term "signing bonus", not every bonus will be paid up front.

2. To woo the top candidate away from competitive firms.
In the race to hire the best and the brightest, the hiring market takes on the aura of a cattle auction, with the best "breeds" commanding as high a bonus as the market will bear. So if your skills are scarce or in high demand, you can expect to see firms up the ante in a competitive bidding war for your talents. Let out a joyful *Mooooo* if you are one of these lucky bovines, because very few are.

3. When the firm cannot pay you the salary you have asked for.
Large companies are often restricted in what salary level they can offer a candidate. Their company policy may dictate set salary ranges for certain experience levels. If you are asking for more than their salary range will allow, they may choose to offer you a generous signing bonus as compensation for the lower salary.

So you should analyze your own bonus in terms of why the firm may be offering it. This will help you understand if the offer makes sense to someone like yourself with short-term employment horizons. If the firm is motivated by Reason #1 above, then the offer is not a good deal for you, since you would leave before you could ever collect the bonus. In this case, you would be better off taking compensation in the form of the highest salary possible.

of pricing and underwriting securities, but not being able to sell the securities to investors).

round lot   A unit of trading—generally 100 shares of stocks and either $1,000 or $5,000 par value in the case of bonds.

safekeeping   The storage of a customer's securities, typically in a vault, provided as a service by a bank or institution acting as agent for the customer.

scenario analysis   An analysis examining the likely performance of an investment under a wide range of possible markets and models.

secondary market   The market for issues previously offered or sold.

sector   The grouping of securities into a category, based upon similar features. Sectors can be defined as nationalities, regions, industry group or other feature.

secured bond   Debt backed by specific assets or revenues of the borrower.

securitization   Securitization may be broadly defined as the process of issuing new securities backed by a pool of existing assets such as loans, residential or commercial mortgages, credit card debt, or other assets.

seed money   Initial funding of a start-up business provided by angel investors. Seed money can take the form of a loan, an investment in preferred stock or convertible bonds, or of common stock, providing the startup with capital needed for early stage development and growth.

senior securities   Securities with a preferential claim over common stock on earnings and in the case of liquidation. Bonds and preferred stock are generally considered senior securities.

selling group   A selling group includes dealers or brokers who have been asked to join in the offering of a new issue of securities, but are neither liable for any unsold syndicate balance, nor share in the profits of the overall syndicate.

sell side   In a securities firm, the part of the business which transacts and executes orders, including the activities of retail brokers, institutional brokers, traders, and research departments.

senior bonds   Bonds considered senior to other bonds within an entity's capitalization structure and which have a higher priority to repayment than another bond's claim to the same class of assets.

share   A share is a unit of ownership in a corporation, mutual fund or partnership. In the United States, the term stock is often used instead of share, although an investor actually owns shares of stock.

shell corporation   A corporation with no assets and no business, typically designed for purpose of acquiring other businesses.

short   Borrowing and then selling securities that one does not own, in anticipation of a price decline.

short-term debt   Generally, debt which matures in one year or less.

sovereign risk   The risk that the government in the country where the bonds are issued will take actions that will lead to deterioration in the bond's value.

speculator   An investor willing to take large risks in return for a large gain, and where the possibility of loss of original principal is a secondary factor.

spread   Generally, the difference between the market price and cost of purchase plus any service fee.

stated maturity   The last possible date on which the last payment of the longest loan may be paid.

stock dividend   A dividend paid in securities rather than in cash. The dividend may be additional shares of the issuing company, or in shares of another company (usually a subsidiary) held by the company.

stockholder of record   A stockholder whose name is registered on the books of the issuing corporation.

stock index futures   Futures contracts based on market indexes; e.g., NYSE Composite Index Futures Contracts.

stock options   The right to purchase or sell a stock at a specified price within a stated period. They offer the opportunity to hedge positions in other securities, to speculate on stocks with relatively little upfront investment, and to capitalize on changes in the market value of options contracts themselves. Also refers to a widely used form of employee incentive and compensation, wherein the employee is given an option to purchase its shares at a certain price (at or below the market price when purchased) for a specified period of years.

stock ticker symbols   A unique identification or symbol of a corporation listed on the exchanges, which can be up to four letters. Many of these ticker symbols have become synonymous with the corporation itself, as in IBM for International Business Machines or ATT for American Telephone and Telegraph.

stop limit order   A stop order that becomes a limit order after the specified stop price has been reached.

stop order   An order to buy at a price above or sell at a price below the current market.

strategic investors   Investors with valuable industry and personal ties that can be used to help the company raise additional capital or obtain industry and marketing expertise.

subscription agreement   The application submitted by an investor wishing to join a limited partnership. All prospective investors must be approved by the general partner prior to admission to becoming a partner.

syndicate   A group of investment bankers who jointly underwrite and sell a new issue of securities.

swap   A transaction in which an investor sells one security and simultaneously buys another with the proceeds, usually for about the same price and frequently for tax purposes.

sweat equity   Ownership of shares in a company acquired by hard work in the enterprise rather than by investing capital per se.

syndicate   A group of underwriters formed for the purpose of participating jointly in the initial public offering of a new issue of municipal securities.

taxable municipal bond   A municipal bond whose interest is not excluded from the gross income of its owners for federal income tax purposes, usually because the underlying project is deemed to lack a broad public benefit.

tax anticipation note (TAN)   Notes issued by states or local governmental units to finance current operations in anticipation of future tax receipts.

tax-exempt bond   Bonds, usually municipal bonds, on which the interest is excluded from the gross income of its owners for federal income tax purposes and which may also be exempt from state and local taxes.

T-bill rate   The weekly average auction rate of the three-month Treasury bill stated as the bond equivalent yield.

technical default   A default under the bond indenture terms, other than nonpayment of interest or principal.

technical research   Analysis of a particular stock based on its supply and demand. To understand these patterns, a researcher would examine price and volume trends.

10-K   A comprehensive report detailing a public company's performance, history, organizational structure, equity, holdings, and earnings per share. It is submitted annually to the SEC.

10-Q   A comprehensive report detailing a public company's performance and general financial position. It is submitted quarterly to the SEC.

tender offer   An offer by one corporation to buy shares from stockholders of another corporation. Stockholders are asked to "tender" (surrender) their holdings at the offered price, usually at a premium above current market price.

third market   Refers to the trading of stock exchange-listed securities in the over-the-counter market.

ticker   A traditional telegraphic system used by historic stock exchanges from about 1870-1970 that provided ongoing price and volume information on all securities trades made on the exchanges.

total bonded debt   Total general obligation bond debt outstanding of a municipality, regardless of the purpose.

total return   Investment performance measure over a stated time period which includes coupon interest, interest on interest, and any realized and unrealized gains or losses.

trade date   The date upon which a bond is purchased or sold.

trader   Individuals who buy and sell for their own accounts for short-term profit. Also, refers to an employee of a broker dealer firm who handles the purchases and sales of securities for the firm or its clients.

tranche   Refers to a segment or portion of an investment issue within an offering in which each tranche offers different terms, such as varying degrees of risk.

transfer agent   The party appointed by an issuer to maintain records of bondholders, cancel and issue certificates, and handle administrative issues related to these records.

Treasury securities   Debt obligations of the U.S. government, including bills, notes, bonds, TIPS, and Savings Bonds. When you buy a Treasury security, you are lending money to the federal government for a specified period of time.

trigger   The market interest rate at which the terms of a security might change.

trustee   An institution, usually a bank, designated by the issuer as the custodian of funds and official representative of bondholders.

U.S. Savings Bond   A nonmarketable bond issued by the U.S. Treasury in face value denominations and designed for individual investors; interest is exempt from state and local taxes and no federal tax is due until bond is redeemed.

underwriter   The securities dealer who purchases a bond or note issue from an issuer and resells it to investors.

unit investment trust   An investment fund created with a fixed portfolio of investments to provide a steady, periodic flow of income to investors.

unsecured debt   Debt with a claim for repayment that ranks last after all other forms of debt securities in the event of a corporate liquidation.

variable rate bond   A long-term bond which has an interest rate that is adjusted periodically based upon specific market indicators.

volatility   The propensity of a security's price to rise or fall sharply.

volume   The number of shares traded in a security (or market) during a given time period. Volume is calculated on a daily basis and a daily average is computed for longer periods.

voting right   The common stockholders' right to vote their stock in company issues. Preferred stockholders will typically have voting rights when preferred dividends are in default.

warrant   A security that entitles the holder to buy a certain amount of common or preferred stock at a specified price for a period of time. Warrants are usually issued with a loan, bond or preferred stock, acting as a sweetener to enhance the marketability of the primary security.

yield   The annual percentage rate of return earned on a bond calculated by dividing the coupon interest by its purchase price.

yield spread   The difference in yield between two bonds or bond indexes.

yield to maturity   The yield on a bond calculated by dividing the value of all the interest payments that will be paid until the maturity date, plus interest on interest, by the principal amount received at the maturity date.

zero-coupon bond   A bond which does not make periodic interest payments; instead the investor receives one payment, which includes principal and interest, at redemption.

Chapter 6

Resources

There is no shortage of information available on careers in the finance industry. The challenge is to sift through the avalanche of books, directories, newsletters, periodicals, and Internet sites to find the best sources. For a career as popular as investment, it is not surprising that a lot has been written about the topic. Consider that 176 million results turn up on a Google search on "financial careers." Unfortunately, not all of the information on the Internet is trustworthy. There is also the danger of relying *too* much on the Internet, forgetting what great resources are available in the "real world"— even in often-overlooked sources like museums of finance. The list below is designed to help you sort through the melee and hone in on what you need as quickly as possible.

Associations and Organizations

Angel Capital Association (ACA) is a trade association of leading angel investment groups in North America. ACA's mission is to offer angels the opportunity to collaborate, network, and exchange information about Individual angels who are accredited investors can join "angel groups." Divided by investment strategy, angel groups serve as networking forums to share information about new venture opportunities. Other activities include advancing the industry through political activities at the state and federal level.   (http://www.angelcapitalassociation.org)

CFA Institute (formerly the Association for Investment Management and Research) is a global organization of investment professionals with a focus on the activities of financial analysts. Its scope is fully multinational with over 101,000 members from 136 countries around the world. The institute administers exams for certification as a chartered financial analyst (CFA) and in investment performance measurement (CIPM). Its Web site offers educational resources on a large variety of investment topics. (http://www.cfainstitute.org)

Futures Industry Association (FIA) is an industry trade group for futures professionals and others in the securities business. FIA publishes a magazine (Futures Industry Magazine) and holds conferences for members. Its Web site is a rich source of articles on financial regulation and reform applicable to the industry. Member firms are listed, along with a link to their Web site. (http://www.futuresindustry.org)

The **Institute for Financial Markets (IFM)** is a Washington, DC-based, nonprofit, educational organization that provides services, products, and information about the industry to both professionals and public policy makers. It is an affiliate of the FIA, with a focus on futures and options. Its Web site is a resource for numerous educational topics, including regulation, best practices, and standards of conduct. The IFM also publishes test materials for the Series 3, 31, 32 and 34 securities exams and holds classes on futures, options, and other topics. (http://www.theifm.org)

Investment Company Institute (ICI) is a trade association of American investment companies, focusing on the fund industry (mutual funds, closed-end funds, exchange-traded funds, and unit investment trusts). ICI's history dates back to the creation of the American fund industry in 1940. Its Web site features a useful directory of investment companies listed by type, with links to their Web sites.

The **International Securities Association for Institutional Trade Communication (ISITC)** is a relatively new organization founded in 1991, ISITC is a cross-disciplinary group of securities professionals who aim to develop standards for better electronic communications and trade processing. Broker/dealers, investment managers, utilities, and vendors comprise the membership roster. Although its focus is technical in nature, membership could provide a rich source of networking opportunities. (http://www.isitc.org)

Managed Funds Association represents firms and individuals in the alternative investment space, which includes hedge funds, managed futures funds and funds of funds. Headquartered in Washington, DC, the MFA does political and advocacy work for the industry at the state, national and international levels. Its members are alphabetically listed on the Web site, and are said to include the majority of the largest hedge fund groups in the world.

The **National Association of Seed and Venture Funds (NASVF),** founded in 1993, is a relatively new organization, bringing together leaders in private and venture capital. Its objective is to "build local economies by investing in local entrepreneurs." Originally founded with a technology focus, the organization has broadened its scope in recent years and is now international, with 775 individual members from four countries. (http://www.nasvf.org)

National Venture Capital Association (NVCA) is a trade association representing the American venture capital industry with about 400 member firms. It has an online membership directory available by subscription. Other resources available by subscription include the annual *Venture Capital Yearbook*, which provides industry statistics and analysis of the industry, among which are the number of new firms and funds, disbursements by industry and state, and data on IPOs and MandAs. Available to nonsubscribers are past issues of several venture capital publications, including *NVCA Today*, a quarterly newsletter; *Venture Impact*, a study of the economic impact of new ventures and *Patient Capital*, a study of new medical ventures in the health care industry.

Securities Industry and Financial Markets Association (SIFMA) is a leading securities industry trade group representing securities firms, banks, and asset management companies in the United States and Hong Kong. SIFMA was formed on November 1, 2006, from the merger of The Bond Market Association and the Securities Industry Association. Its Web site offers extensive industry research, statistics, and reports that cover economic and political issues. Recent regulatory changes are examined for their impact on the securities industry. (http://www.sifma.org)

Security Traders Association (STA) is a historic organization formed in the aftermath of the 1929 stock market crash, at a time when new securities laws were being passed to address the problems that had led to the collapse. Today, its activities revolve around political action on behalf of the industry. Members are individuals involved in equity and debt trading, rather than institutions or firms. (http://www.securitytraders.org)

Books and Periodicals

These print resources will help you position yourself in your career.

Books

Seek out some of the following books to get a more well-rounded take on the financial industry.

Biographies

Charles Schwab: How One Company Beat Wall Street and Reinvented the Brokerage Industry. By John Kador (Wiley, 2002). More than just a personal biography of a entrepreneurial legend, the book tells the story of the birth of discount brokerages and how they revolutionized the securities business in the 1970s. Along the way, readers will gain insight into how the securities industry operated from the 1970s to the present.

Hetty: The Genius and Madness of America's First Female Tycoon. By Charles Slack (Harper Perennial, 2005). The author attempts to restore the sullied reputation of one of America's least known Wall Street tycoons. Hetty Robinson Green (1834-1916) was a Massachusetts woman who parlayed an inheritance into a major fortune through shrewd investments in post-Civil War bonds and greenbacks. This book looks at the personal and professional life of the so-called "Witch of Wall Street."

The House of Morgan: An American Banking Dynasty and the Rise of Modern Finance. By Ron Chernow (Grove, 2010). This biography sets out to show how the Morgan family created the J.P Morgan banking house and assesses its impact on the United States and European financial systems in the past two centuries.

The Life and Legend of Jay Gould. By Maury Klein (The Johns Hopkins University Press, 1997). The author probes into the legendary career of the Gilded Age financier, finding more to the story than the "robber baron" tag commonly associated with him. An interesting revisionist history about a key figure in American business.

Soros on Soros: Staying Ahead of the Curve. By George Soros (Wiley, 1995). Told by the famed Hungarian-born investor himself, this book recounts his personal life story, as well as his investing theories and philosophies. He expounds on the founding of the Quantum Fund and other investment tales. The story is told in interview style, with questions asked by journalist Krisztina Koenen and J. P. Morgan Stanley investment strategist Byron Wien.

The Tycoons: How Andrew Carnegie, John D. Rockefeller, Jay Gould, and J. P. Morgan Invented the American Supereconomy. By Charles R. Morris (Holt, 2006). The book tracks the storied careers of four legendary men from the Gilded Age, weaving their personal stories against the backdrop of 19th century American financial history. An absorbing look at how four investors contributed, for better or worse, to the rise of the American economy.

General Interest

Basic Black-Scholes: Option Pricing and Trading. By Timothy Falcon Crack (Timothy Crack, 2009). While there is nothing really basic about the Black-Scholes model, this book is an attempt to explain it in elementary terms for general readers. Whether you are an industry professional, a mainstream investor, or just preparing for a job interview, this book will give you a good refresher course on options pricing models.

The Essays of Warren Buffett: Lessons for Corporate America. By Warren E. Buffett and Lawrence A. Cunningham (The Cunningham Group, 2008). Written by the Oracle of Omaha himself, this is a lively and informative compendium of Buffett's annual Letters to Shareholders and other writings. A great introduction to the investment theories and practices of a legendary figure.

An Introduction to Investment Banks, Hedge Funds, and Private Equity: The New Paradigm. By David Stowell (Academic Press, 2010). This book is an academic, but relevant treatment of the investment and private banking industries. It deals with recent trends and changes in industry structures and practices in light of recent regulatory reforms.

One Up On Wall Street : How To Use What You Already Know To Make Money In The Market. By Peter Lynch and John Rothchild (Simon and Schuster, 2000). Written by a well-known Fidelity Investments fund manager and research analyst, this book explains how the man on the street can use common sense and everyday knowledge to make winning stock picks. Good advice for both professionals and amateurs.

A Random Walk Down Wall Street: The Time-Tested Strategy for Successful Investing. By Burton G. Malkiel (W. W. Norton, 2011). An investment guide to the market using the principles of behavioral finance. A well-known book on portfolio strategy, using principles of psychology to understand market behavior. The author discusses many types of investments, including stocks, bonds, insurance, real estate, gold and collectibles.

Security Analysis. By Benjamin Graham, David Dodd (McGraw-Hill, 2008). The classical and classic work on value investing. Along with Graham's other work, The Intelligent Investor, the book is recognized as one of the most important works ever written about the value-investing strategy.

Wealth Management: The Financial Adviser's Guide to Investing and Managing Client's Assets. By Harold Evensky (McGraw-Hill, 1997). A professional's guide to the art of financial planning that covers asset allocation policies for clients in different circumstances and life stages. The book offers practical advice for structuring a client's portfolio in accordance with his personal long-term goals. Recommended by Charles R. Schwab.

License Preparation and Study Guides

Since securities laws change frequently, be sure to buy the most recent edition of the study guide. Here is a sampling of some of the Series 7 guides available. Also available are guides for the Series 6, 65 and 66 exams.

Barron's Stockbroker Examination: Series 7 (Barron's How to Prepare for the Stockbroker's Examination Series 7). By Michael T. Curley (Barron's Educational Series, 2007).

NASD Stockbroker Series 7 Exam: Preparation Guide. (Compass Learning System), Cengage South-Western (2003).

Pass the 63: A Training Guide for the FINRA Series 7 Exam. By Robert Walker (First Books, 2010).

Novels

L'Argent (Money). By Emile Zola (Mondial, 2007). Zola's take on the life and times of a mid-19th century French speculator. Along the way, you will learn plenty about France's economy and stock market.

The Financier. By Theodore Dreiser (University of Illinois Press, 2010). This classic book, first published in 1912, was the "Wall Street" of its day. Unlike the 1987 movie, however, The Financiers is an eminent piece of literature told by a master novelist. Dreiser's book is a devastating portrait of an unscrupulous financier who will go to any length, including crime, for money and power. The book is noteworthy for its portrayal of the preregulatory era of American financial history.

The Pit: A Story of Chicago. By Frank Norris (Wilder Publications, 2010). Published in 1903, this novel deals with commodities speculation at the Chicago Board of Trade at the turn of the twentieth century when the concept was still fairly new. The "pit," of course, refers to the Board's trading pit. If you are interested in the early futures market, this book is a lively read, as well as an outstanding piece of classical literature.

Shark Out of Water: A John Putnam Thatcher Mystery. By Emma Lathen (HarperCollins, 1998). One of a series of financial/murder mysteries about John Putnam Thatcher, an investment banker who solves crimes. Light and entertaining fare by the writer who has been called "The Agatha Christie of Wall Street" by the *Los Angeles Daily News*.

The Velocity of Money: A Novel of Wall Street. By Stephen Rhodes (Avon Books, 1999). A financial thriller involving a mysterious suicide, threat of a capital market meltdown, a prominent investment banking firm, and a conspiracy to drive stock prices down using automated trading programs.

Zero Coupon. By Paul Erdman (Forge Books, 1994). One of nine books about the money markets written by a former banker who turned to fiction while in a Swiss prison awaiting trial on charges of fraud. Erdman was an early practitioner of the now-common literary form known as the "financial thriller." In addition to the usual adrenaline thrill of the genre, his books offer a painless way to learn about the intricacies of international finance. His other novels include *The Silver Bears, The Swiss Account,* and *The Billion Dollar Sure Thing.*

Periodicals

Barron's and Wall Street Journal has been published by Dow Jones and Company since 1921, Barron's Magazine is a weekly financial publication in paper form, with an online edition. It offers analysis and in-depth commentary on American financial markets and is more objective in approach than most publications covering the financial markets. (http://online.barrons.com) Another

Everyone
Knows

Wall Street Animal Farm

The investment world has its own quirky terms, under-stood by no one but them. Here are a few examples from the animal kingdom.

Viper Refers to Vanguard Index Participation Equity Receipt Shares, a series of funds offered by the Vanguard Group

T-Rex Slang for a very large and powerful venture capital fund.

Elephants Slang for the large institutional investors whose high dollar trades can have a major impact on market prices.

Goldbugs An investor who is bullish on gold and invests in it frequently.

Cockroach theory A Wall Street term that refers to the idea that one disclosure of negative information about a company means that more bad news will be forthcoming, just as the sight of one cockroach usually means more are hidden in the woodworks.

Colts Short for "continuously offered longer-term securities," colts are sold by the World Bank and can be either fixed rate bonds, variable rate bonds, or zero-coupon bonds.

Dow Jones publication, the *Wall Street Journal*, offers a daily dose of in-depth financial and business reporting covering the globe, though with a focus on U.S. topics.

The Bond Buyer is the daily newspaper of the municipal bond market. It was founded in 1891. The Bond Buyer publishes news stories, new-issuer calendars, results of bond sales, notices of redemptions and other items of interest to public finance professionals. Especially helpful is a current list of industry conferences and events across the country. (http://www.bondbuyer.com)

The Deal Magazine is the self-described "Voice of the Deal Economy," a magazine is for professionals in private equity, M&A, hedge funds, and venture capital. Its affiliate is *The Deal Pipeline* (http://www.thedeal.com), an information service providing transactional information about current deals in the market.

Gazelle A company or stock with sales in excess of 20 percent per annum.

Deer market A slow market, characterized by low trading volumes and seemingly timid investors.

Black swans Random and unpredictable events that impact the stock market.

Bulldogs A bond issued in Britain by a foreign company, typically denominated in British pounds.

Dog and pony show Refers to financial seminars or conferences that present new securities products or investments to potential buyers.

Gorilla A company that dominates its sector or industry, such as Google.

Cats Short for "catastrophe bond," a high-yield, insurance-backed bond containing a provision causing interest and/or principal payments to be delayed or lost in the event of loss due to a specified catastrophe.

Dead cat bounce No relation to the cat bond, a dead cat bounce is a temporary recovery (or bounce back) from a bear market, after which the market continues to fall.

Institutional Investor is a family of international financial publications for an institutional audience, including Institutional Investor Magazine (monthly paper magazine with online edition), Institutional Investor Research (information on research, trading, investor relations and other industry topics), Institutional Investor newsletters for specialty groups within the securities industries, AR Absolute Return + Alpha (covering hedge fund industry) and several others. Especially helpful are their periodic rankings of America's "best," from money managers to sell-side analysts to research teams. (http://www.institutionalinvestor.com)

Investor's Business Daily was first published in the 1950s. It is the investment daily newspaper provides information on company, stock, and industry trends. Readers can expect a daily dose of

Looking for a Hedge Fund Job?

You have got your MBA, but do not know where to start. How does one break into the notoriously hard-to-crack hedge fund industry? Do not expect the résumé alone to land you an interview—you will probably need more than that. Not only are the best jobs rarely advertised, competition is fierce for the few available slots. To break into the industry, you will need superior skills and iron determination. Start out by learning the ropes of the industry. Learn the lingo of the business. Stay up to date on industry performance, trends, and players. Find out "who's who" in your chosen area. Consider an internship to get your foot in the door, or, if you have skills in other fields, offer your services as a consultant. Stake out conferences and seminars where hedge fund managers might hang out. And of course, network, network, network.

stock tips and ideas in both the print and online editions (the digital edition by subscription only). (http://www.investors.com)

Money Management Executive is a paper and online publication for executives of the money management industry, including those involved in mutual funds, hedge funds, separately managed accounts, and other alternative investments. It publishes news affecting the entire money management industry, as well as compliance, marketing, sales, operational, and legal coverage. (http://www.mmexecutive.com)

The MoneyTree Report is a quarterly study of venture capital activity in the United States presented jointly by PricewaterhouseCoopers, Thomson Reuters, and the National Venture Capital Association. The site offers a wealth of current and historic data, trends and statistics on the venture capital industry. Historic data is available beginning in 1995. Quarterly data is organized by industry, state, and venture capital firm. (http://www.pwcmoneytree.com)

Red Herring was started in 1993 at the dawn of the Internet boom. The magazine is devoted to the financial and business side of technology. It is a great source of trends affecting investments in technology companies, although somewhat less relevant than it was in the 1990s at the height of the Internet boom. (http://www.redherring.com)

Business School Rankings and Listings

Bloomberg Businessweek publishes annual rankings of MBA and undergraduate business programs. Its Web site has a "Business School Comparator" tool that can pull up information on schools by selected criteria. (http://tools.businessweek.com/BSchool_Comparator/)

Forbes ranks business schools granting MBA degrees by several criteria, including name, location, five-year gain, salary, and GMAT scores. It also has a ranking of the best foreign schools. (http://www.forbes.com/2009/08/05/best-business-schools-09-leadership-careers_land.html)

Princeton Review, an independent educational organization, ranks business schools by eleven different classifications, including best administered, best professors, and "Toughest to Get Into." (http://www.princetonreview.com/faqs-business.aspx)

Smart Money's Best Colleges for Making Money, although published at the end of 2008, is still relevant to ranking today's education market. It provides a cost/benefit analysis of a college education, comparing alumni salaries with tuition and fees at 50 major universities. The results were surprising: some public universities ranked higher in terms of "payback" than many elite private schools. The top-ranked schools were University of Texas at Austin, Georgia Tech University, and University of Georgia, all with higher "payback-ratios" than Ivy Leaguers like Dartmouth, Yale, and Harvard Universities. For additional details, see the slideshow at http://www.smartmoney.com/Personal-Finance/College-Planning/The-Best-Colleges-For-Making-Money.

U.S. News and World Report surveys 426 business schools for its annual ranking. (http://grad-schools.usnews.rankingsandreviews.com/best-graduate-schools/top-business-schools/rankings)

Other Media

Plan your next career move and some constructive downtime with the following resources.

Films

The Bank (2001)   An Australian version of the financial thriller, this is the saga of a deviant mathematician who devises a way to predict the vagaries of the stock market.

Boiler Room (2000)   An independent film in the film noir genre about a college dropout who gets a job at an investment brokerage house to please his father. The movie presents the ethical dilemmas and legal problems the protagonist faces as he rises up the career ladder.

Clancy in Wall Street (1930)   While financial thrillers may be the genre of choice for modern movies about Wall Street, during the Great Depression the preferred format was the "financial comedy." This is a representative example of the genre, about a plumber working at a stock exchange who "accidentally" buys some stocks on margin. The trouble begins when the fellow becomes a millionaire, then a pauper, in quick succession.

Dealers (1989)   The film takes place at the London branch of American investment bank in the aftermath of a major loss of $100 million and the suicide of a top trader. It depicts the London financial scene during the Thatcher era, and has lots of interesting though overblown details about the world of currency traders.

Pi (1998)   The tale of a lonely, reclusive mathematician who applies his computational genius to the stock market and finds he has stumbled on the secret to predicting its behavior. Along the way, he is pursued by a Wall Street firm that demands (at gunpoint) to know his secret trading formulas. A cross between a financial and a psychological thriller.

Quants: The Alchemists of Wall Street (2010)   An unusual documentary about the mathematical wizards who invented the financial models that Wall Street lives by. A rare look at the professors, techno-geeks, and software programmers whose work has had a profound influence on the modern stock market. The film is available on the Web at http://www.youtube.com or at http://www.businessinsider.com/wall-street-movies-2010-9#quants-the-alchemists-of-wall-street-2010-10.

Trading Places (1983)   This is another film in the "financial comedy" genre that unites Eddie Murphy, Dan Akroyd, and Denholm Elliott in a tale of two commodity brokers who wager a bet that they can turn a petty criminal into a successful businessman.

Museums

Bureau of Engraving and Printing is the federal agency that produces our nation's paper money supply, and has two facilities available for public tours. In both the Washington, D.C., and Fort Worth, Texas, locations, visitors can watch real money being printed from above the production floor. (Washington, DC: 14th and C Streets, SW, Washington, DC 20228, 877-874-4114; and Fort Worth: 9000 Blue Mound Road, Fort Worth, TX 76131, 866-865-1194, http://www.bep.gov)

Museum of American Finance is located in the heart of New York's financial district. The museum offers exhibits that chronicle the nation's financial history. "The Financial Markets" exhibit is a multimedia display that gives visitors a history of the district's colorful past. The Museum also has a quarterly magazine, a lecture series, and an archive. (48 Wall Street, New York, NY 10005, 212-908-4110, http://www.moaf.org)

Web Sites

The following Web sites are excellent resources for career changers of all experience levels.

Career Web Sites

Careers-in-finance.com offers a wealth of valuable information about different segments of the financial services industry, including salary information, career trends, job descriptions, skills in demand, and more. A job bank is also available. (http://www.careers-in-finance.com)

Career-journal.com is a general career site based in Germany that is distinguished by the global scope of its international job bank. The searchable listings are not limited to finance, but cover many industries. (http://www.career-journal.com)

eFinancialCareers.com is comprehensive Web site devoted to every type of financial career. The site has job listings from 22 countries around the world, making this an essential tool for the job seeker looking for international opportunities. In addition to job listings, the site has the usual mix of news, salary surveys and career tips and advice. For entry-level candidates just out of school, there

Professional Ethics

The Chinese Wall

The cornerstone of professional ethics for investment bankers is the avoidance of conflicts of interest. If an investment bank is engaged in several types of activities, such as research, sales/trading and private/investment banking, then management must impose an information blackout between the departments. Called a "Chinese wall," the rule was first defined in the 1930s following the Great Depression, and was strengthened with the passage of the Sarbanes-Oxley Act of 2002. Examples of abuses include situations where equity analysts generate favorable reviews of a company in order to develop relationships that will lead to highly profitable investment banking business. Still another abuse occurs where sell-side analysts are motivated to draft positive research on a company for the sole purpose of selling stocks, IPOs, or otherwise manipulating market prices. Not only are these practices illegal, the laws are becoming stricter and are more enforced today than ever before. To keep your career on the up and up, avoid all conflicts of interest and be sure you fully understand your responsibilities under the law.

is an eFinancialCareers Student Centre. (http://www.efinancial-careers.com or http://www.jobsinthemoney.com.)

Financialjobbank.com is an industry niche job board for the finance industry, part of the Beyond.com network of career sites. The site includes lots of job categories (such as accounting and information technology) irrelevant to securities professionals, but investment jobs can be found with a targeted search. (http://www.financialjobbank.com)

Financejobboardnetwork.com is an online association of job boards pertaining to finance. Its online membership list is useful for job-seekers looking for some of the smaller, specialized or regional job boards across the United States. (http://www.financejob-boardnetwork.com)

Financial Job Network is job and career site for finance professionals, offering job listings from around the world. Additionally, you can find listings of business schools in the United States and in selected countries around the world, largely from Europe, Canada, and Australia. (http://www.fjn.com)

Financejobs.net is a general-purpose career site for financial professionals, complete with job bank. (http://www.financejobs.net)

MMEcareers.com is a career site for money management executives. A searchable job bank is available. The site is affiliated with the finance industry publication, *Money Management Executive*. (http://www.mmecareers.com)

Monster.com and Careerbuilder.com are great places to start your general job search. Below are some other sites that offer specialized job listings tailored to the finance and securities industries. (http://www.monster.com) (http://www.careerbuilder.com)

Mutualfundcareers.com actually covers a broad array of job categories, including mutual funds, general investments, money management, banking, hedge funds, operations, finance, sales, and financial analyst. (http://www.mutualfundcareers.com)

WSJ.com/public/page/news-career-jobs.html is a career site run by The Wall Street Journal and accessible by link from the online newspaper at http://www.wsj.com. A fully international job bank is available. (http://online.wsj.com/public/page/news-career-jobs.html)

Directories

Directoryofinvestment.com is a directory of investment resources, including lists of venture capital and money management firms. This site even provides links to other directories. A valuable resource for jobseekers. (http://www.directoryinvestment.com/bonds/research-and-analysis.html)

The Private Equity and Venture Capital Directory is an online directory managed by an English company, PSEPS Ltd. In addition to providing lists of venture capital and private equity firms, the directory provides names and contact information for limited partners, associations, and individuals. The lists include names from all over the world. (http://www.pseps.com)

Wall Street Executive Library offers general business links and others are more specialized links to finance and investment. Its government, research and news sections conveniently link you to a variety of global sites. The site is especially strong in Canadian financial listings. (http://www.executivelibrary.com)

General Web Sites

Businesshistory.com is an informational and educational site devoted to general business history; its Wall Street link has a large number of resources for students of Wall Street history. (http://www .businesshistory.com)

Hoover's is the classical resource for U.S. company profiles and financial statements. In electronic form, the listing is more useful than ever. A limited amount of information is available for free, but to get the complete listing, you will need to pay for a subscription. Especially helpful are the industry profiles, which include a set of "call preparation questions" that will prepare you for interviews. (http://www.hoovers.com)

Hoover's IPO-Central lists information about current IPOs. Like the main database, this listing offers some information for free, but a subscription is required for more detailed information. It also provides IPO calendars and performance information. (http://www .hoovers.com/ipo-central/100004160-1.html)

IPOmonitor.com is an online subscription service that offers detailed information about current initial public offerings and secondary equity offerings. The service includes pricing alerts, daily email reports, searchable databases, custom report generation, and data and statistics. (http://www.ipomonitor.com)

Library.hbs.edu is the online portal to the vast resources of the Harvard Business School Baker Library at Bloomberg Center. Unfortunately, most of the site's resources are accessible only by students and faculty of Harvard. Nevertheless, one can learn a great deal about available resources just by reviewing the links listed on the site. Consider using the site to identify sources, and then use your local library to access them. (http://www.library.hbs.edu)

Moodys.com is the Web site of Moody's Investors Service, a leading provider of quantitative credit ratings and research on debt offerings, covering debt issues in over 110 countries. (http://www .moodys.com)

SEC.gov/EDGAR is the portal to most of the public company filings of the SEC. EDGAR, the Electronic Data Gathering, Analysis, and Retrieval system, allows anyone to review financial information on public companies. It is also the automated acceptance system that allows companies to file forms and documents with the SEC. (http://www.sec.gov/edgar.shtml)

Wetfeet.com is an online career resource guide, and not just for those with "wet feet." Founded by a pair of Stanford MBAs in the 1990s, the site provides everything the novitiate needs to know about finding a career: industry and company information, nailing an interview, negotiating a compensation package, plus other things. Its sister site, (http://internshipprograms.com) offers information on summer intern opportunities, internships abroad, and more. (http://www.wetfeet.com)

Educational Resources

MBA Program
Booth School of Business
University of Chicago
5807 South Woodlawn Avenue
Chicago, Illinois 60637
http://www.chicagobooth.edu/fulltime

MBA Program
College of Management
Georgia Tech University
800 West Peachtree Street
Atlanta, Georgia 30308
http://mgt.gatech.edu/mba/index.html

MBA Program
Darden School of Business
University of Virginia
100 Darden Boulevard
Charlottesville, Virginia 22903
http://www.darden.virginia.edu/web/Home/

MBA Program
Harvard Business School
Harvard University
Soldiers Field
Boston, Massachusetts 02163
http://www.hbs.edu/mba

MBA Program
Kenan-Flagler Business School
University of North Carolina
CB 3490, McColl Building

Chapel Hill, North Carolina 27599-3490
http://www.kenan-flagler.unc.edu/programs/mba/index.cfm

MBA Program
Marriott School of Management
Brigham Young University
W437 Tanner Building
Provo, Utah 84602
http://marriottschool.byu.edu.mba

MBA Program
Mendoza College of Business
276 Mendoza College of Business
University of Notre Dame
Notre Dame, 46556, Indiana
http://business.nd.edu/mba/

MBA Program
SMU Cox School of Business
Southern Methodist University
P.O. Box 750333
Dallas, Texas 75275
http://www.coxmba.com

MBA Program
Stanford Graduate School of Business
Stanford University
518 Memorial Way
Stanford, California 94305-5015
http://gsb.stanford.edu

MBA Program
Stephen M. Ross School of Business
University of Michigan
701 Tappan Street
Room E2540
Ann Arbor, 48109-1234, Michigan
http://www.bus.umich.edu

MBA Program
Tepper School of Business

Carnegie-Mellon University
5000 Forbes Avenue
Pittsburgh, Pennsylvania 15213
http://www.tepper.cmu.edu

MBA Program
Wharton School
University of Pennsylvania
420 Jon M. Huntsman Hall
3730 Walnut Street
Philadelphia, Pennsylvania, 19104
http://www.wharton.upenn.edu/mba/admissions/index.cfm

Index

S

salary, signing bonus *versus*, 124–125
Sarbanes-Oxley Act of 2002 (SOX), 17, 50
Savings Bond, U.S., 129
Schapiro, Mary L., 74
Schiff, Jacob, 16
Scholes, Myron, 21. *See also* Black-Scholes Model
Schwab, Charles, 19–20, 134
Searles, Joseph, 18
SEC. *See* Securities and Exchange Commission
securities
    brokerages, 30–31
    gray list, 65
    lending fraud, 43
    SEC-registered, 42
securities, commodities, and financial services sales agents (BLS 41-3031), 38–39. *See also* commodities exchanges
Securities Act of 1933, 17, 40–42
Securities and Exchange Commission (SEC), 40
    regulatory accountants and, 75
    securities registered with, 42
    Web site, 43
securities compliance examiner, 75–77
Securities Exchange Act of 1933, 17
Securities Exchange Act of 1934, 42–43
securities industry
    FINRA and, 54
    regulatory framework of U.S., xvi
Securities Investor Protection Act of 1970, 45–51
Securities Investor Protection Corporation (SIPC), 45–50
    insurance, 49–50
securities trading
    early experiments in, 1–3
    history, 7
securitization, 126
self-regulatory organizations (SROs)
    registration, 42
    regulation, 42–43
sell-side, 126
    research analyst, 73
senior bonds, 126
Series 3, 52, 55–56

Series 6, 55
Series 7, 55
Series 30, 52
Series 31, 52
Siebert, Muriel, 18
signing bonus, salary *vs.*, 124–125
SIPC. *See* Securities Investor Protection Corporation
social investors, 46
socially responsible companies, identifying, 47
socially responsible investing (SRI), 46–48
    changes in, 48–49
    job market, 49
SOX. *See* Sarbanes-Oxley Act of 2002
SRI. *See* socially responsible investing
SROs. *See* self-regulatory organizations
state regulators
    enforcement staff, 77
    inspections and compliance staff, 77–78
stockbrokers, retail, 80–82
Stockerblog (http://stockerblog.blogspot.com), 41
Stock Exchange Luncheon Club, 19
stock exchanges
    European, 9–13
    history, 5–6
    mergers and acquisitions of, 21–22
    U.S., 13–14
stock indices, celebrity, 41
stock markets
    crash, x
    crash of 1929, 16–17
    crash of 1987, 21
    European, 5–7
    global, 9–14
    regulated, 17
    U.S., 7–8
stock trading
    commissions, 8, 19–20
    electronic, 19–20
    rigging of, 8

T

Telecom, media, and technology bubble. *See* TMT bubble
tender offer, 42, 129
terminology, xvii, 138–139